THE ART OF FLINT KNAPPING

FOURTH EDITION

Written by D.C. Waldorf
with illustrations by
Valerie Waldorf

TABLE OF CONTENTS

"MOUND BUILDER BOOKS"
P.O. BOX 702
BRANSON MO 65615

INTRODUCTION

"Truly, stone is a much more subtle and flexible material than it appears to be...with considerable practice almost anybody should be able to learn to make simple tools. He will not make very good ones. He will not make them with the speed and virtuosity of Francois Bordes, the French prehistorian who has made a specialty of this craft...and he will certainly make nothing that Homo-Erectus would have been proud of. In fact, today's would-be tool maker can only be impressed by the enormous skill that every ancestral craftsman must have had."

These words appear in the book *Early Man* by F. Clark Howell (Howell 1965:105). It was one of the first volumes of the Time Life Nature Library and was, no doubt, one of the first widely distributed publications to contain a small section on making stone tools which could serve, though incomplete, as an introduction to flint knapping. There have been other writings on the subject, but this is the one that I found first and it has left me with a lasting impression. The statement, "He will certainly make nothing that Homo-Erectus would have been proud of" was a challenge. I vowed that I would someday be as skilled at making stone tools as had been my ancestors. The photo essay in that book showing Professor Bordes at work making a hand axe and a laurel leaf was a real inspiration for a 16 year old kid trying to chip arrowheads out of the bottoms of beer bottles. Little did I realize that this would lead to more than 25 years mastering the art of flint knapping.

Francois Bordes and his American counterpart Don Crabtree, who did the first scientific studies on the replication of Folsom points, are both gone now. It is to their memory that this edition is dedicated. They were the first to bring the art of working stone out of the darkness of time. Although in the past there have always been commercial knappers working anonymously, because of their secrecy they have made little impact. It would be the likes of Crabtree and Bordes who would become the pioneer fathers of lithic technology. We, the second generation of 20th Century knappers, will always stand in their shadow.

Ironically, my love of chipping would lead me to become a commercial knapper. However, I was too proud of my accomplishments to keep quiet about them. It is my strong belief that the knowledge of flint

FIG. 1.   Type III Danish dagger made by D.C. Waldorf from Pedernales chert, 12 & 5/8" long. Daggers of this type were made just prior to the Bronze age, circa 1900 B.C. The most prominent characteristic on the square sectioned handle is the "stitching".

3

working is a part of our human heritage, it is the one thing that all the races of man the world over, have in common. If you could trace your ancestors back far enough you would certainly find flint knappers among them.

The first edition of *The Art of Flint Knapping (Waldorf 1975)* was suppose to be a simple booklet explaining how the Indians made their arrowheads with some instructions on how to make your own. This publication was to be sold in conjunction with flint knapping demonstrations that I used to give, and it also helped promote my work. As time went on, the second and then a third edition came to reflect a growing need for more precise and technical information.

As the author has matured in his craft, so flint knapping has grown to become an accepted tool of research by experimental archaeologists trying to uncover the past by recreating it. Knapping, meanwhile, has grown much faster as a hobby with literally thousands of practicioners at various levels of competence. Therefore, this fourth edition was designed with them in mind while still retaining much of that which made it such a popular text with professionals. Since the greatest number of these books are destined for distribution in the United States and Canada, the content mostly deals with biface production as it is found in the North American archaeological record. Some old world core and blade technologies along with gunflint production will also be covered because they are relevant to the study of the art.

Before continuing, it must be mentioned that no matter how good this book or any other book on the subject might be, there is still no substitute for continuous practice or a natural aptitude for manual skill. The importance of hands-on experience cannot be stressed enough: the more you chip, the more you learn. If you are fortunate enough to witness a demonstration put on by a master knapper, pay close attention. You can learn so much that it may advance your progress by a year or more.

Today we can still master the skills of our ancestors and maybe even surpass them.

Good luck and good chipping,

D.C. Waldorf

FIG. 2. The Type IV Danish dagger is the ultimate challenge for the modern flint knapper. This specimen was made by D.C. Waldorf from Ft. Payne chert, 10 & 1/4". With their flaring handles, these were copies of bronze weapons that were being traded north from the Aegean. The Type IV reached its final development around 1800 B.C.

Chapter 1
SOME PRELIMINARY QUESTIONS

This first chapter and the one that follows are based on some of the many questions put to the author by those who were unfamiliar with flint working. The answers to these questions will serve to introduce the subject to the novice.

Where did the term "flint knapping" originate?

In England, a flint knapper was one who made gun flints. Gun flints are those little square pieces of flint which are inserted into the hammer of a flintlock rifle. They are necessary for striking a spark which causes the powder in the pan to ignite the charge in the barrel.

However, we must go to Germany to find the roots of the term. The German word "knapp" can mean to crack, pinch off, or to nibble, which describes the action of the flint knapper as he pecks off flakes with his hammer. There is another German word which among many things has come to mean workman or craftsman. This word is "knappen". Though both knap and knappen are different in meaning they can both relate to working flint in that one describes the action and the other refers to the person who does the action.

In addition to language there is another reason to believe that the term originated in Germany. The Germans were the first to develop the flintlock rifle. In those days the art of working raw flint into gunflints was a closely guarded secret. With the spread of the flintlock rifle the secret became known: England and France took over the gunflint business.

The same principles involved in making gunflints were used by prehistoric man in making tools and weapons. Therefore anyone who works in flint, both modern and prehistoric, can be called a flint knapper.

Didn't the Indians heat their flint and drop water on it to chip it?

Of all the questions asked I think this is number one on the list. It deals with an old myth which I believe will never die out completely. Some people have come to me swearing that they have heard of or even seen an eighty year old Indian who could make an arrowhead this way. Knowing the facts, it is easy to understand how this theory got started. Years ago when Indians were first corralled on reservations, they were often visited and studied extensively by anthropologists and other curious white men. Most if not all of these Indians had already entered the Iron Age and had forgotten flint knapping in the span of two or three generations.

However, some of the old timers who knew of the process wanted to keep this last vestige of their culture a secret, and so created the myth of using heat and water. Thus, the white man walked away satisfied and the Indian was left alone to brood and have a quiet chuckle. Around the turn of the century this story became so well accepted that even most of the Indians believed it.

As this legend lived on into the 20th Century it was again to surface in the ever popular writings of Edgar Rice Burroughs. Chapter Three of *The Beasts of Tarzan* (Burroughs 1914) provides a lengthy description of how Tarzan made a knife using this method. Who knows how many people have read this passage and accept it as fact?

When I was eight years old I held a handful of arrowheads in wonder and asked myself, "How could the Indians make implements out of stone so hard that it could scratch glass?" For many people it is easy to see the effects of heat and water as elements of Nature, so why didn't early man, living so close to Nature, imitate her? With experimentation, it is soon found that when acting on flint, these elements are uncontrollable. Flint, being a fine grained rock, will crack and check when heated and suddenly cooled. Large masses of the stone will explode, making this process a very dangerous one. (Heat treating, which will be discussed later, could also have been misunderstood or confused with chipping by fire. They are not the same thing as you will soon see.)

If the Indians didn't use heat, how did they work their flint?

The surface of an arrowhead when closely examined, will exhibit a wavy appearance. These "scars" are a frozen record of shock waves generated by a series of blows dealt to the flint.

Geologists tell us that flint has a conchoidal fracture, which is best illustrated when a BB strikes plate glass. A "cone" of glass is removed opposite the point of impact. When striking the edge of a piece of flint using a hammerstone or deer antler, only a portion of that cone is removed. By controlling the angle and weight of the blows it is possible to fracture flint in a predictable manner.

In making his implements, prehistoric man used one or a combination of three techniques which are known as: percussion flaking, indirect percussion, and pressure flaking.

Percussion flaking: Flakes are driven off by striking the edge of the flint with a hammerstone or deer antler.

Pressure flaking: Flakes are pried off with an antler tine, copper or mild steel tool.

Indirect percussion: Flakes are removed by an antler or metal punch placed on the edge. The butt of the punch is struck with a hammerstone, antler billet, or wooden maul.

Why use a deer antler for percussion flaking? Wouldn't a steel hammer work better?

There really isn't any material that is equal to a deer antler for percussion flaking, however, there are several fairly good substitutes which will be discussed in the chapter dealing with tools. The reason antler works so well is that as it hits the edge of the flint it is soft enough that it sticks for a fraction of a second. This concentrates the force of the blow and releases its energy slowly, thus producing a wide, flat flake. A steel hammer, on the other hand, has no give. It releases its energy too quickly, resulting in a crushed edge with many step fractures. A metal hammer may be useful in breaking up large blocks of flint and for the manufacture of gun flints, but for making arrowheads the deer antler works much better.

If a metal hammer doesn't work for percussion flaking, then why does a metal tool work for pressure chipping?

In pressure chipping no blows are dealt, instead constant pressure is applied until a flake pops off. For applying this pressure anything harder than your fingernail will work. Deer antler tines are good, but I prefer to use a copper pointed tool because the metal point is tougher and doesn't require as much resharpening as does antler. Many commercial knappers find the use of metal pressure flakers also more desirable because less time is wasted in the resharpening of tools. Under certain conditions, however, there is a difference in flake scar attributes when an antler flaker is used as opposed to a copper flaker. If the copper tool is kept very sharp, the negative bulb will be more defined. Should the tool be allowed to dull a bit, the scars will be shallower like those made with an antler. These differences are very minor, but should be kept in mind if one wishes to do a 100% accurate replication. Prehistoric people who are thought to have used copper tools were the Neolithic Danes, some of the Mound Builders in the midwestern U.S., and the people of the Archaic Old Copper Culture of Michigan and Wisconsin.

How long does it take to make an arrowhead?

Using the methods that I will show you in the upcoming chapters, an experienced flint knapper can make a common two inch projectile point in 15 to 20 minutes. Larger spears and knives will require much more time depending upon the type of point being made, the technique used in manufacture, and the individual knapper. It can take anywhere between one hour to possibly all day. I have made some pretty nice 4 to 5 inch spears in two hours. Making a Danish dagger requires from 6 to 24 hours depending upon the type.

Other factors that might be considered along with the production time are heat treating (24 to 72 hours), and down time, that is, the time spent resharpening tools, resting between chipping sessions, or the time required to study over a problem that has developed.

What is heat treating?

"Thermal alteration of lithic materials" or heat treating is a simple process that produces some astonishing results. The toughest, meanest cherts can be tamed and made to work and look like the highest grades of flint when they have been placed in the ground under a hot fire. In the next chapter I will show you how to cook the hard cherts, thus helping you exploit marginal resources. We will also study the structure and occurrence of lithic materials.

Can one tell the difference between arrowheads made today and those made in ancient times?

It is very difficult to tell the difference, especially when the point is "made right". That is, if it is a true replica of a common flint type made by an experienced flint knapper working in the traditional manner. In this case the only thing a collector can do is examine the piece for wear and patina. Unfortunately, even these can be duplicated by an unscrupulous person, thus adding to the difficulties of identification. This can be prevented to a certain extent by marking the points using a carbide tipped engraving tool. All that is needed is the maker's initials and a year date. But, even this is not foolproof; the engraver can also undo what has been done or a patch of heavy patina can be conveniently placed over the marks.

If you are collecting and wish to purchase artifacts, knowledge is your best weapon against fakes. It requires years of study and handling of authentic artifacts in order to get "the feel" of the genuine article. Know your types and the regional variations of those types. Know your raw materials and how each patinates under natural conditions. Attend "knap-ins" and watch knappers work. There you will notice the differences in their styles. The more you understand about flint knapping and how these items are made, the less susceptible to fraud you will become.

What contributions can flint knapping and the knapper himself make?

The obvious contribution that the commercial knapper makes when he sells his work in the open is more objects for the collector to collect. The scarcity of better quality artifacts has driven their market value sky high, 'way out of the range of the average person, so it's only natural that such items be placed back in production. Hopefully, in the future the collecting of modern works will help to reduce pot hunting. The mining of archaeological sites by untrained persons looking for valuable items has reached epidemic proportions in this country.

Aside from creating a new aspect of collecting, the potential contributions to archaeology are enormous. Many students are learning to chip so they will have a better understanding of what they are dealing with when flint artifacts are retrieved from a site. With fewer and fewer undisturbed sites to excavate, many researchers are turning to making and using replicas of artifacts in order to learn more about them in a direct way. The field of experimental archaeology is growing and many of the better knappers in this country are professional and amateur archaeologists. Now and in the future, we can expect from them some great discoveries as they work to increase and enrich our knowledge of the past.

Flint knapping as a hobby is good therapy. I know many people who chip for fun and relaxation while some hobbiests sell their work, with most of the profits going to offset the cost of obtaining flint and tools. As far as making a living as a knapper, if you have a choice you'd be better off choosing something else. When chipping for bucks, knapping has just the opposite effect of therapy. Take it from one who has been there. It's rough on the muscles as well as the nerves, and there is always the danger of silicosis.

What is silicosis?

Silicosis was probably man's first industrial disease. The gunflint makers in England suffered from it, and the full time commercial knappers of the late prehistoric period no doubt had similar problems. Some of the silica dust produced when flint is broken can get into your lungs and stays there. Like billions of tiny razor blades, these dust particles lacerate the tissues of the air sacs forming scar tissue which causes loss of elasticity and the ability to absorb oxygen. Usually the victim dies of pneumonia, tuberculosis, or other complications. This disease takes a long time to develop, maybe ten to fifteen years, depending upon the amount of exposure and whether or not the person already has some other respiratory disorder. Smoking is also a major factor. The only way to halt the progress of silicosis is to stop exposing oneself to silica dust. The bad news is that unlike other lung ailments, the effects of this one are irreversible.

The best and most convenient way to lessen your exposure is to work outside where the wind can blow the dust away. If you have to work inside, ventilate the area with a fan in the window. Work only when you don't have to run a forced air furnace or an air conditioner. Because the dust is so fine, it will go through the filters into the ductwork, spreading throughout the house and exposing other members of the family as well. Also, about 25% of this dangerous dust is produced by abrading edges for platform preparation. Keeping your abrading stone wet by placing it on a moist sponge in a plastic tub will eliminate virtually all of the dust produced from this operation.

For those who are considering flint knapping as a business let me add these suggestions. If you have to work inside from time to time, use a building separate from your home. Make sure it is well vented. Take a shower and change your clothes immediately after work and consider wearing a respirator. One type can be purchased from the Mine Safety Appliances Co. in Pittsburgh, Pennsylvania. Ask for information about their COMFO 2 Custom Respirator with filter cartridges for asbestos containing dust, fumes, and mists. The thing looks a lot like an old WW 1 gas mask minus the eye piece. The only trouble I have had is that it covers the nose in such a way that it makes wearing my glasses difficult. By the way, those disposable dust masks for sale in hardware stores are of little or no value for filtering silica dust and fumes.

While much has been made of the dangers of silicosis, the non-smoking part-time knapper who works outside or in a ventilated shop has other dangers to worry about such as deep cuts, eye damage due to flying debris, and damage to muscles and tendons due to overexertion or overuse. All of these injuries can be prevented with protective equipment and common sense. As you read through this book the emphasis will be on safety.

Where can one go to meet other knappers?

In the past few years knap-ins have become quite common. These are annual or bi-annual gatherings that take place at historical sites or are hosted by individuals on private property. The largest and best known of these are the spring and fall knap-ins at Ft. Osage in Missouri and one that is held in the spring near Killeen, Texas.

Chapter 2
FLINT, FLINT SOURCES AND HEAT TREATING

Flint is a form of quartz *(SiO2, silicon dioxide)*, one of the most abundant minerals on Earth. Flint does not have an ordered crystal lattice like pure quartz and other minerals. It is cryptocrystalline: the quartz crystals are microscopic in size, randomly arranged, and cemented together by a matrix of impurities. Because of its structure, flint doesn't fracture along cleavage planes as does a crystalline material. Its fracture is conchoidal due to the molecular bonds being equal in any direction.

Technically, the so called "flint" that is to be found in the United States is really not true flint. Most of it comes under the heading of chert as well as other minerals from the quartz family, such as chalcedony, jasper, agate, and so on. We flint knappers have a tendency to lump all of the lithic materials we work, except for obsidian, under the generic term of flint. This keeps it simple.

What is the difference between flint and chert and where are they found?

According to what I've read and heard, true flint is found in chalk beds that were formed during the Cretaceous period. It comes in nodular form, is black, grey or brown in color, opaque or semi-translucent, and about 99% quartz. Examples of true flint are to be found in the chalk beds of England, Denmark and other locations in northwest Europe. In the United States the closest thing to true flint that I am aware of are nodules found in a chalk formation that is a member of the Austin Limestone deposit of central Texas.

Chert is found in association with limestone and dolomite deposits and sometimes in association with sandstone and shale. It is considered an impure form of flint, about 90% quartz. Most chert is grey or white, however, it can be any color or a combination of colors, and occurs in three basic forms: nodules, lenses, and beds.

Nodular chert is found in balls or irregular masses in chalk or limestone. Most nodular flints and cherts are of high quality with colors ranging from light grey to black, brown, or a combination of these colors in bands or swirls. All of these nodules are protected from the weather by a chalky scale or **cortex**. This cortex, or "bark", as some local collectors call it, varies in thickness from 1/4 to 1 & 1/2 inches. Nodules can be the size of an egg up to 15 or 20 inches in diameter with the average falling between 6 and 12 inches.

Lens chert is found in lens-shaped deposits seen as an ellipse in the face of the outcrop, the exposed surface being a cross-section of the lens. Actually, lenses are very large, flat nodules and will often have many cracks which allows the flint to come out in square or rectangular blocks. Lenses are also covered with a thin cortex which may still adhere to one or both ends of the detatched block. For the most part lenses are larger than nodules. They can be from three feet across or as long as an automobile, and from one inch to over a foot in thickness.

Bedded chert, the most massive of all deposits, appears as a solid layer in the parent rock, from less than 1 foot to as much as 50 feet in thickness. The deposit could be 100 feet or 100 miles long.

What is obsidian?

Obsidian is a volcanic glass that is found in the volcanic regions of the Rocky Mountains and the Sierras. Most obsidians are black, some are translucent, while others have a green or purple metallic sheen. Mahogany obsidian has a brown coloration which makes it resemble the wood after which it is named.

Obsidian was formed by the rapid cooling of lava. Its composition is similar to other igneous rocks such as granite. It is a mineraloid, not a true mineral because it is amorphous (having no crystalline structure). Obsidian fractures at the molecular level producing some of the sharpest edges known to man. Due to this property it works much easier than flint and is a favorite of amateur knappers.

What about some of the other lithic resources?

Chalcedony, jasper, agate, fossil replacements, and man-made glass are some of the other materials available to the modern knapper.

Chalcedony is a group term for a waxy, smooth form of quartz that is usually found lining cavities, filling cracks, or forming crusts. It is often transparent, but more often translucent with the most common colors being white to grey, blue, brown or black. Members of the chalcedony group include: carnelian, red in color; sard, a brown to honey color; chrysoprase, a rare green variety, and agate with alternating bands of color.

Jasper is a mineral similar to flint. It is opaque and has a high iron content which gives it a characteristic red, orange, or yellow color. Chalcedony, agate and jasper are not only found in sedimentary rocks, but also in layers of basalt which is volcanic in origin. In this case the silicates are concentrated in voids or spaces between the layers by water percolating through the stone.

Fossil replacements occur where organic matter has been buried by sediments or lava flows and ash falls. The once living organisms were slowly replaced by silicates that turned them to stone, often preserving details such as grain in the case of petrified wood. Most petrified woods are found in volcanic rocks with the exception of palm wood from Louisiana.

Another fossil replacement that is a well known lithic resource is agatized coral, heavily used by the Indians of central Florida. Horribly tough and grainy, it is found in solid and hollow coral heads. The coral polyps may still be visible in the stone which is white, grey, or tan. Although a few high grade pieces can be worked in their natural state most have to be heat treated, considerably improving the flaking quality.

When all else fails and one gets desperate for a lithic fix, there is always the ubiquitous beer bottle. I have made some mighty fine "Old Milwaukee points" from beer bottle bottoms. Colored store front glass is fun if you can find it and will make some very large spears. You might consider stained glass that can be had from a hobby store carrying supplies for this craft. Also, anyone who makes stained glass windows or lamps will have pounds of scrap pieces usually in triangular shapes, perfect for making small points. Slag glass from an old factory is a challenge because it comes in irregular chunks very much like natural lithic materials and must be reduced in the same manner. All in all, if you choose to work glass the colored or opaque varieties are the best because you can see the pattern of the flake scars more easily.

If one wishes to try his hand at working flint, how could he go about finding a good source of raw material?

The first thing that should be done before going into the field is a search of the archaeological literature that has been written about your state or area. In such books and papers one may find references to raw materials used by the local Indians. If the chert bearing formations are named, the next thing to do is get a hold of a U.S. Geological Survey map showing the outcrops. The County Extension Office usually has these maps and can tell you where to get your own.

The formations on these maps are color coded and are keyed to a side bar that shows them in a vertical column, oldest and deepest at the bottom and youngest at the top. If there are little, oval-shaped black dots marked in these layers, the formation has chert in it, and the amount is indicated by the frequency of these dots. You might find that the chertiest layers are of poorest quality. Those layers that have fewer nodules may be of high quality because the silicates

are more concentrated. Streams and roads are shown on the maps, and you should check out roadcuts, ravines, and gravel bars that cut through the chert bearing formations. Any construction that requires excavation may turn up residual nodules in the soil. Some of my best chert sources are in cities rather than in the woods. Also try to avoid prehistoric quarries where you might contaminate an archaeological site with your debitage. Believe me, road cuts and construction areas are much more productive.

Another source of information may be local Indian relic collectors, rock hounds, or a professional archaeologist who lives or works in your area. If and when you find some stone and it turns out to be one of the tougher grades of chert, try heat treating.

What does heat treating do to the stone?

There are two theories based on experiments: one by Barbara Purdy and H.K. Brooks of the Florida State Museum (Purdy and Brooks 1971), the other by J. Flenniken and Ervan Garrison of the University of Arkansas (Flenniken and Garrison 1975). Purdy and Brooks claim that the matrix of impurities around the quartz crystals melts and reforms into a denser material that holds the quartz crystals more firmly. This would permit the shock waves to travel not only around the quartz crystals, like they do before heat treating, but through the crystals as well. When the shock can go through the medium unobstructed it will go farther, producing longer, thinner flakes. The gain in density would mean less energy is required to drive off a flake, making the job easier.

On the other hand, Flenniken and Garrison claim that instead of reforming the matrix the heat causes microfracturing of both matrix and crystals. Micro-fracturing occurs when the matrix and the crystals, being of different composition, expand at different rates. This expansion causes stress in the stone which is relieved by microscopic fracturing that does not destroy the stone, but merely weakens it enough to permit a gain in workability.

It must be noted that Purdy and Brooks used Florida cherts while Flenniken and Garrison used Arkansas novaculite which is a form of quartzite. There is quite a difference between these two; novaculite heat treats at a higher temperature, (800-950 degrees F.) while the Florida cherts that I have worked with will heat treat at lower temperatures, (550-650 degrees F.). Depending on the material, both of these theories could be right.

What is the procedure for heat treating?

Today most commercial knappers and a lot of serious hobbiests have gone to using modified pottery kilns not only for the convenience, but because some live in cities where open burning is banned. These appliances have an infinite temperature control and a built in pyrometer. The control allows you to raise the heat at any rate desired, and the pyrometer tells you what the interior temperature is. Some of the more expensive kilns now have computer controls so the rate of temperature rise, hold and fall can be programed. Otherwise, you have to stay home and check it every once in a while and fiddle with the dials. However, this little inconvenience is nothing compared to stoking a hot fire in the dead of summer.

The procedure for heat treating in a kiln is simple. Just stack your blanks inside and fill up the box with those which cook at the same temperature. No sand bath is required, but some people use a metal box that just fits inside the kiln. This prevents the sharp edges of the preforms from doing damage to the soft fire bricks that line the interior. After the lid is closed, the heat is raised at 75 to 100 degrees F. per hour until the critical temperature is reached. This will vary for different stones and experimentation may be necessary. As a general rule, all cherts heat at below 1000 degrees F. and most between 400 and 600 degrees F.

If you're blowing up blanks the temperature is too high, the rate of heat increase is too fast, or the stone is too wet and may need a drying cycle. For this cycle I set my dial on low and leave it overnight. By morning the temperature is about 300 degrees F. Holding at or just above the boiling point for 6 to 12 hours will dry the stone and the temperature can be safely raised.

Some cherts may require only one hour at the critical temperature, or as long as two or more hours, after which the power is turned off for those in the 650 degree or lower range. Some kilns cool faster than others, and it may be necessary to back the temperature down slowly for those materials in the 650 and above range. This procedure prevents thermal shock caused by rapid cooling. Usually at or below 500 degrees it is safe to shut down. The door can be opened when the pyrometer reads 150 degrees F.

What evidence has been found to support the theory that the Indians knew about heat treating, and is it possible to duplicate their methods?

The best evidence that I can cite is that which I discovered myself upon moving to Missouri. At first I found it difficult to locate a large source of high grade material. About 50% of the artifacts in the area were made from a beautiful, lustrous white and pink chert. For two years I searched for the source. It was just about this time that a relic collector from Kansas City and several other knappers that I met suggested that I try heat treating. So I went back to the hillsides above the campsites where I found various outcrops of white chert. I took some home and proceeded to conduct

my own experiments, and sure enough, the old white chert took on a new luster and color that was identical to that found on the Indian campsites. I know for certain that this is the same material the Indians used because the same fossils that appear in the unheated chert from the outcrops appear in the finished artifacts.

Heat treating in the ground is as much an art as it is a science, and I learned a lot through experimentation. First of all, it can be accomplished under very primitive circumstances if the conditions are right. With an unlimited supply of dry brush and small logs (2 to 4 inches in diameter) a run can be made with no difficulty, providing the ground is not soaking wet and you can be assured of a 10 to 15 MPH breeze for at least twelve hours.

First dig a flat bottomed pit about 6 inches deep, throwing the dirt up around the edges. It can be 2 to 4 feet across depending on the number and size of the blanks you have. Then a small "drying fire" is built in it. (If the ground is very dry this step may be unnecessary). The length of time the drying fire is kept burning depends upon how long it takes to dry out the ground under it, usually from 2 to 4 hours. After the fire has done its job it is smothered by an inch or so of soil from the rim. Now the blanks are placed in and covered by another 1 to 1 & 1/2 inches of soil, all of which is packed down by stepping on it. The firmly packed dirt will dry out quickly if it is still moist and will transfer the heat to the blanks more efficiently than loose soil. The remaining dirt at the edge of the pit should be mounded up to form a rim 3 or 4 inces high, helping to contain the coals.

Now the primary fire can be built by adding wood as fast as it will burn to make charcoal. The idea is to have a bed of charcoal at least 4 to 5 inches thick built up in the pit after 6 to 8 hours of feeding. With a ten MPH breeze this will burn all night long. It should be stirred well before you go to bed and if there is not enough fuel then more should be added.

If everything goes well and the fire burns hot and evenly all night, it should still be hot and smoldering at dawn with only a small amount of charcoal left. However, if the pit is cooler than you think it should be or there is a lot of unburned charcoal left then it may be necessary to reburn in order to be certain that the proper temperature has been reached. To reburn, simply stir up the coals, start a new fire and run it for a couple of hours. Then let it go. After a number of runs, both failures and successes, you will know instinctively when things are right and what to do if not.

The cooling period lasts for about two days. Usually the morning of the third day after the fire was started it is safe to remove the ashes. If the ground is still too hot to lay a hand on, then let it cool until afternoon before digging the blanks out. Don't try peeking at a single blank when you know that the dirt is still too hot!

Breaking the seal lets the heat escape from the pit more rapidly. This can cause some of the blanks in that area to break!

While people worry about overheating, I have found that most failures result from not getting the fire hot enough or from too rapid cooling. If executed properly this method will produce some very high temperatures, some reaching 650-700 degrees. I know this for a fact because I have cooked stone that turns glossy at these temperatures in an electric kiln.

For those who live in town where there might be a ban on the open burning of wood or brush, you might try the method I first described in the 1979 edition (Waldorf 1979:12 &13). If you add a grill and cook a steak, the fussy neighbor next door will think it's a new-fangled barbeque pit.

The set-up is a very simple one, consisting of the bottom third of a 55 gallon drum buried in the ground and filled with eight inches of sand. I have a sheet of steel that serves as a rain cover to keep the sand dry when the pit is not in use. Otherwise, you not only have to heat the sand, but dry it too. This takes a lot more fuel and time. Wet sand can easily be dried by spreading it out on a flat surface in the hot sun. Extra sand should be kept on hand to replace that which is lost with the ashes when they are removed.

When I want to heat treat I remove the first inch of sand, then I pack down the remainder by walking on it. After the blanks are laid in and pushed down so that their upper faces are all at the same level an inch or so of sand is poured back on and packed down.

I usually start the fire at nine o'clock in the morning with ten pounds of charcoal and a lot of charcoal lighter. The day should have some breeze to produce the maximum amount of heat. After about two hours I pour on five more pounds. Additional five pound lots are added every two hours or so until twenty or thirty pounds have been reached. The size of the pit, what you intend to cook in it, and the amount of air moving will determine the amount of charcoal that you need. With a little bit of experimentation, you will have no trouble at all determining the proper charge. Turn the coals about once every half hour until all of the charcoal has been added. After the last five pounds little stirring is done as this causes a heat loss. At nine or ten o'clock the next morning I scrape off the ashes leaving the sand alone to cool. At noon or whenever I can touch the sand without getting burned, the blanks are removed.

I like to do a series of runs as it is difficult to attain the highest temperatures in the first run. Successive runs heat up the sand and the ground all around the pit. In the first run I place agates, agatized coral, Alibates, Edwards and other materials that do not need a higher temperature. In the following runs I put the harder materials into the sand which is still warm from the previous firings.

If I plan to make only one run I place the easier to cook blanks around the outside edge, and the largest, toughest blanks in the middle where the heat is more intense. I may also throw on an extra five pounds of charcoal to make sure everything gets done. Using the 55 gallon drum and briquets I can barely reach 600 degrees (with a lot of wind). This is fine for Texas flints and some local cherts. With this in mind I started to experiment with a combination of the old Indian method and the steel lined pit.

I got hold of an old, oval-shaped wash tub (2 by 4 feet by 1 foot deep), buried it in the ground, filled it with sand to within 5 or 6 inches of the rim, and stoked it with wood just like the Indian pit. Some people use old cast iron bathtubs, either buried or above ground. There are several advantages that this hybrid method has to offer. First, it stays dry because the sand is contained and covered with a sheet of tin when not in use, eliminating a drying fire. Secondly, the bathtub capacity is double that of the drum. Third, with ten acres of woods around me the fire wood is no problem and much cheaper than store bought charcoal briquets. I have also burned a lot of construction debris, such as ends of 2 X 4's and timbers from old houses that were torn down.

Can a person use the oven in his kitchen for chert which heat treats at a lower temperature?

I have successfully heat treated a lot of Georgetown flint (350-400 degrees F.) and San Antonio chert (up to 500 degrees F.), as well as other low temperature materials using this procedure:

1. Place the stone to be heat treated in a **covered** metal pan, a turkey roasting pan is ideal. The lid will protect your glass oven door should a blow-up occur. No sand bath is necessary.

2. Start heating by setting the temperature on its lowest possible setting for at least 1/2 hour. In an electric oven this may take longer.

3. Increase the temperature by 50 degrees per hour until the maximum temperature is reached. Leave it on this maximum temperature for at least 1 hour.

4. Turn the oven off and allow it to cool naturally with the oven door closed.

I do not recommend using this method for materials that require 500 degrees plus. Some of the newer ovens are made of lighter, thinner steel than the old ones and cannot sustain temperatures at the highest settings for prolonged periods without warping some of the internal parts or the door.

Do not attempt to heat treat rocks in a micro-wave oven! They heat up too fast causing great stress in the stone. Therefore they blow up and can damage the appliance.

Before closing this chapter I wish to add a few more random comments and helpful hints.

When most lithic materials reach "critical", that is the point at which alteration occurs, they become very sensitive to sudden temperature and pressure changes. If you have enough control over the fire you can lessen your breakage rate considerably by not going too far beyond the critical temperature and stress can be minimized by not throwing logs in, but placing them in gently.

If you have been successful your blanks should come out whole with some color change, and having a smooth, glossy or waxy texture when flaked as opposed to the duller, original surface. When they come out in pieces and the fracture surfaces are glossy then your blanks were overheated or they cooled too quickly. Those that are dull, but have some color change, and are still tough, didn't get hot enough. On some materials color change may occur before the critical temperature is reached, so color cannot always be accepted as an indicator of successful heat treatment. Only changes in luster and a gain in workability are acceptable. If any blanks are unsatisfactory they can be reheated in the next run.

In a wood or charcoal fire temperatures can be controlled somewhat by the amount of fuel you use and by the rate at which it is fed. The depth at which you bury your blanks is an even better control; closer for hotter, deeper for cooler. This will require some experimentation to determine the proper depth, usually no closer than 1 inch and no deeper than 3 inches. You can also increase the efficiency of the operation by putting in two layers of blanks, one at 1 inch below the fire and another under that at a depth of 2 to 3 inches from the surface. In the upper layer are those that take the highest heat while the bottom layer is shielded and will reach a much lower temperature. A good example would be Flint Ridge chert over Texas chert.

Wind speed, air and ground temperatures are also factors to be considered. A warm, dry day with a temperature of 70 degrees or higher and a 10 to 15 MPH breeze is ideal. I will also take advantage of a 90 degree day in the middle of summer when the ground temperature may be 80 degrees. This will add to the heat already generated by the fire.

If a sudden storm comes up it will usually contain strong winds that will fan the flames. If you are using wood just build the fire up. By doing this I once saved a hundred prime blanks from a real howler. Fortunately they were in my washtub pit which kept the ground water out. If it is a charcoal fire or in the ground, unless

you are a lucky person or find some way to cover the pit and still allow the fire to burn, you might as well write it off.

I don't like to cook rocks in the dead of winter because you have to heat up the frozen ground and the blanks cool off too quickly as the fire dies. While you're cutting wood for the winter you can also lay in a flint supply by using the dry tree tops from last year's cutting to fuel this year's heat treating fire.

Thermally altered stones have their advantages and disadvantages: that which is easy to make is easy to break. A sack full of colorful, heat treated blanks may be a boon for the commercial knapper, but will they hold an edge if made into woodworking tools or heavy duty butchering knives? The student of lithic technology has to look at the archaeological record to find clues as to the design and use of stone tools. This is something to consider if one wishes to make true replicas of those tools.

If the decision is made not to heat treat there is another way in which some workability may be maintained or gained. I noticed that when the tougher grades of Flint Ridge chalcedony were first quarried they were easier to work. As they dried out flaking became somewhat more difficult. Maintaining a stone's freshly quarried moisture content or restoring it by keeping the preforms submerged in a bucket of water is referred to as **water treatment.** I have found that this works best on true flint, such as Danish or British flint, Georgetown flint, Pedernales tabular chalcedony, and other varieties of chalcedony. Gains in workability are from 0.5 to 1 on the lithic grade scale.

The Lithic Grade Scale as devised by Callahan (Callahan 1979:16) goes from 1: very brittle, glass-like materials to 5: tough, grainy, almost unworkable stones like rhyolite and felsite. Most of the materials favored by mid-west knappers fall into the 1 to 2.75 range. Personally, I like those between 2.5 and 3 because they pattern well when worked with the billet. If I plan on a lot of pressure work then I will choose those below 2.75. However, the sources in my area that yield such high quality stones are limited, while there are tons of it in the 3 to 4 range, so heat treatment is a necessity.

On the following page is a partial listing of some of the lithic resources used by me and other knappers. They are placed in order of workability as they are found raw. There are hundreds more, some yet to be discovered, but this should give you some ideas. Note: when I say, "Needs no heat treatment", I mean it. These materials are not affected by heat or are ruined by it. The temperatures I recommend were calibrated in my kiln. Pyrometers on other kilns may vary as much as 25-50 degrees. You will have to experiment, and while experimenting use small pieces at first so nothing very valuable is lost if failures occur.

LITHIC RESOURCES

COMMON OPAL AND OPALIZED WOOD. Washington and Oregon. Multi-colored with the predominant color being brown, tan or white. Opaque. 0.75. No heat treatment necessary.

MAN MADE GLASS. Beer bottle bottoms and store front glass. Any color. 1. No heat treatment necessary.

OBSIDIAN. Oregon and California to Colorado and Idaho to Arizona. Black, mahogany and brown. Transparent to opaque. No heat treatment necessary.

PITKIN CHERT. Arkansas. Black. Opaque, 2.25. No heat treatment necessary.

HORNSTONE. Indiana. Nodular chert. Grey and sometimes banded. Opaque, 2.25. No heat treatment.

KENTUCKY BLACK. Kentucky variety of hornstone. Nodular chert. Blue black, opaque. Also a variety that is bluish in color is known as "Kentucky blue". These are all Wyandott cherts from the same formation as the Indiana hornstone. 2.5. No heat treatment.

DONGOLA (COBDEN). Illinois. Nodular chert. Grey to brown and frequently with concentric banding. Opaque. 2.5-2.75. No heat treatment.

UPPER MERCER (COSHOCTON). Ohio. Black or mottled blue black. Opaque. 2.5-3. No heat treatment.

FLINT RIDGE CHALCEDONY. Ohio. Predominately grey, tan and brown. Semi-translucent. 3-3.5. Water treatment will keep it at 3. Heat treat at 550-600° F. Lithic grade is 2.5 after heat treatment.

FLINT RIDGE CHERT. Ohio. Multi-colored. Opaque. 3-4. Better grades will respond to water treatment. Heat treat at 600-650° F. Grainier varieties can go to 675° F. Lithic grade is 2.75 after heat treatment.

ALIBATES. Texas. Multi-colored, predominately red, purple, cream and white. Opaque. 3-3.5. Heat treat at 450-500° F. Lithic grade is 2.75 after heat treatment.

KNIFE RIVER FLINT. South Dakota. Brown to dark brown with occasional cream colored cattail leaf fossils embedded. Semi-translucent to opaque. 3. Heat treatment is tricky, 450-500° F.

DANISH AND BRITISH FLINTS. Nodular. Grey to black. Opaque to semi-translucent. 3-3.5. Water treatment improves the workability approximately 1/4 lithic grade. Heat treating is possible but very tricky, 350° F.

GEORGETOWN. Texas. Grey nodular flint. Opaque. 3-3.5. Finer grades, no heat treatment. Some can be heated at 350-400° F. Grade after treatment is 2.75.

BELTON - FT. HOOD. Texas. Grey to tan. Opaque. 3-4. Depending upon the material, heat treat at 450-650° F. Lithic grade after heat treatment is from 2.5-2.75.

PEDERNALES. Texas. Tabular and nodular. Brown, opaque. 3.25-4. Tabular material can be tricky, try 350° F. Do not exceed 500° F. For nodular material use 340-550° F. Improves to 2.5-2.75 with heat treatment.

HARVESTER. Missouri. Nodular chert. Cream colored with brown banding. Opaque. 3-3.25. Water treat or heat treat at 550-625° F., no higher. Lithic grade after heat treatment is 2.75-3.

BURLINGTON. Missouri, Illinois and Iowa. White or cream colored, tan and gray. Opaque. 3-3.5. Finer grades can be water treated. Heat treat at 650-675° F. Lithic grade after heat treatment is 2.5-2.75.

CRESCENT. Missouri. White or grey. High Ridge variety is multi-colored red, pink, purple and tans predominant. Opaque. 3-3.5. Heat treat no higher than 650° F. Lithic grade improves to 2.5-2.75.

FLORENCE A (KAY COUNTY). Oklahoma. Light tan to grey with numerous white fusilinid fossils. Opaque. 3-3.5. Heat treat at 600-650° F. Lithic grade improves to 2.5-2.75.

NOVACULITE. Arkansas. Predominately white to light grey, or multi-colored. Some black is known. Opaque to semi-translucent. Varies from 3-4. Most black cannot be heat treated. Other varieties heat at 750-900° F.

ONONDAGA. New York and Ontario. Black to grey mottled. Opaque. 3-3.5. Water treatment will help 1/4 lithic grade. Heat treatment does not help or ruins it.

FT. PAYNE. Tennessee. Black to brown, light tan, some varieties have purple banding. Nodular. Opaque. 3-4. Do not heat treat the black varieties. Banded and lighter colored varieties will take 500-675° F. Improves from 3-2.5.

AGATIZED CORAL. Florida. Light grey to white, yellow and orange. Semi-translucent to opaque. 4. Heat treat at 600-675° F. Improves to 2.75.

FLORIDA CHERT. Florida. Yellow to tan. Opaque. 4. Heat treat at 600-650° F. Improves to 2.75.

Chapter 3
TOOLS OF THE TRADE

Let us examine the tools of the trade. These are hard and soft "percussors", pressure flakers, pressure notchers, punches, abraders and protective gear.

Hammerstones or hard percussors were the first and simplest of flint working tools. They were just water worn pebbles of various materials that fit the hand well. They were used to break up nodules and blocks of flint into workable spalls and to rough out large blanks as well as for making pebble tools and hand axes.

To find a good hammerstone prehistoric man followed a creek bed and looked for rounded pebbles that were similar to the ones shown in Fig. 3. I carry at least three hammerstones in my tool kit: a large 4 to 5 pounder (A), a medium one weighing 1 to 2 pounds (B), and a small one of 8 ounces (C).

There are hard hammerstones and soft hammerstones each having a different effect on dissimilar grades of lithic materials. Hard hammerstones are tough chert cobbles or dense quartzite pebbles, granite, or greenstone. The soft ones are of slate, limestone, sandstone or other softer stones. The hard ones are good for heavy work such as breaking up nodules, but the softer ones will act more like antler billets. Some of the better flint knappers that I know who use these tools can actually do a lot of the finer work that I do with the billet, so if you want to save some wear and tear on those precious antlers you might consider this. With a little searching and experimentation you will find the hammerstone that is right for you.

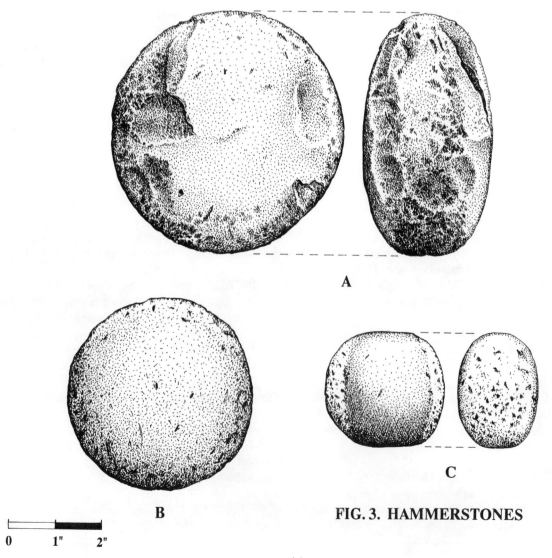

A

B

C

FIG. 3. HAMMERSTONES

0   1"   2"

The antler billet is the most important tool in my flint working kit. I do over 90% of all percussion flaking with it, thinning, shaping, beveling, sharpening and primary retouch. It can also be used to strike the punch for indirect percussion. Shown in Fig. 4 are antler billets used by the author and other well known flint knappers.

The large billet (A) is made from the trunk of a moose antler weighing between 1 & 1/2 and 2 pounds and is used for very heavy percussion flaking. Medium billets (B) are made from smaller moose racks. The weight is from 12 ounces to a pound. The smaller billets (C) are made from the antlers of India stag, white tailed deer, elk antlers and the large tines off a moose antler, they weigh 4 to 6 ounces. Elk antlers are not my first choice because they are light and spongy inside for most of their length. Only the first inch or so near the rosette is solid enough to hold up.

The India stag trunks are used for knife handles and are getting expensive and harder to find. The best places to look for antlers of all kinds are at gun and knife shows, black powder shoots, flea markets, taxidermists, and gun shops handling muzzleloading supplies. At knap-ins there are people who sell moose antlers and other knapping supplies. Ordering antlers by mail from some of these outfitters is possible, but it is always better to go through a whole box full at the store in order to find the longest and heaviest ones. Also, look for the newer, "green" ones. Those that are old and bleached are worthless, except for moose, which seem to get a lot harder and better with age.

After you have found a suitable antler, cut off the trunk for your billet, Fig. 6-A. Billets can range in size from a moose 2 X 8 inches to a white tail 1 X 5 inches. The rounded working end of the tool is formed by grinding the rosette down into a hemisphere. In order for the tool to function properly it must be kept in this shape. If it becomes badly battered, pitted or worn flat in places it will cause hinging and other problems. Most of the wear on my tools is caused by constant "tuning" rather than the actual working. This is the price I have to pay for speed and accuracy, however, I don't throw away large diameter moose billets when they become too short. I simply reduce their diameter by sawing and grinding, thus recycling them into smaller tools. For example, the little billet shown in Fig. 4-C was as large as Fig. 4-A when I started using it several years ago.

In the past there have been many attempts to find substitutes for antler billets. From my own experience I can tell you that there is only one substitute that I have found to be satisfactory. This is a billet made from G-10 fiberglass. Though it weighs just a little more than antler and is a bit more durable, it behaves identically. All platform preparations and strokes are the same as they would be for antler. The only drawback is that it puts off some odor when in use, and one should wear a dust mask when grinding it on the disk sander or belt sander. Because it is made with glass fibers breathing the dust can be hazardous.

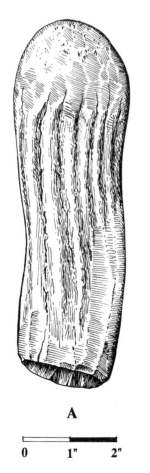
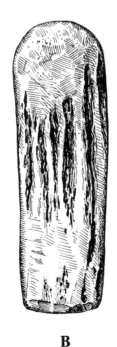

A   B   C   D

0   1"   2"

FIG. 4. ANTLER BILLETS AND PUNCH

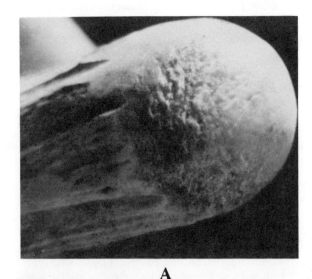

A

B

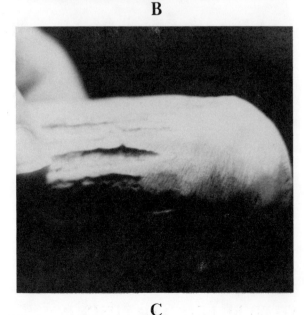

C

Another substitute that has cropped up recently is the copper billet. A large scale commercial knapper in the Kansas City area started using one about 15 years ago. Since then many others have adopted this tool and about 75% of all the knappers in the midwest use it to one degree or another. It consists of a length of copper rod anywhere from 4 to 8 inches long and from 1/2 to 2 inches in diameter. The big 2 X 8 inch ones are used for spalling and billets of 3/4 to 1 X 5 inches are used for general work. I have had no experience using these tools. However, I understand that the platform preparations are slightly different and that the tools take some getting used to. I know that if you begin with copper it is hard to switch to antler, or vice versa, because there is so much difference in the feel.

The way I see this, personally, I don't think the average knapper will be able to get the cleanness and fineness of work that can be done with an antler. Besides, these billets tend to aggravate any tendonitis or tennis elbow conditions that the user may have. The only argument that copper has in its favor is that it's supposedly cheaper and you can get it at any metal supply company. From time to time I may use a fiberglass billet, but for as long as the antler supply holds out, I can recycle my larger horns into smaller ones without ever using copper billets. Therefore, this book is oriented towards antler. If you wish to learn more about copper billets, go to a knap-in and see one in use.

Antler pressure flakers are made from the longest and straightest tines found on the rack, Fig. 6-B. These are naturally pointed to start with, but must be kept sharp while working. Most flint knappers carry a file or rasp in their tool kit for this purpose. For those who have trouble getting deer antlers, or don't like the inconvenience of resharpening them constantly, copper pointed pressure flakers are a good substitute. The tool I use has an antler handle made from a tine with the center drilled out to receive a four inch long piece of copper ground wire, 3/16 inch in diameter, Fig. 7-A. Two set screws in the side near the end of the handle hold the wire in place. As the copper point is resharpened the screws can be loosened and more wire pulled out. When the section of wire gets too short another is inserted. This flaker is a very efficient tool and the one illustrated has served me well for the last 18 years. A similar tool can be made using wood or metal for the handle. Recently someone has been

FIG. 5. When a billet becomes worn and pitted it will cause chattering and hinging, making clean flake removals difficult, A. Antlers can be reground with a power grinder or in this case, with an auto body sander, B. A properly ground billet should be nicely rounded with no flat areas, C.

producing such tools with nylon handles. Also, "Ishi sticks" have become quite popular. These are copper pointed pressure flakers with extended handles from 18 inches to about 2 feet in length. They are held under the arm and are suppose to increase leverage.

Authentic pressure notchers are made from the upper part of the rack or from the thickest tines. Only the hard, outer portion of the antler is used for the point of the tool. By cutting the antler as shown in Fig. 7-D, a good, stiff, durable notching tool can be made. Also shown are metal-pointed antler handled notching tools, one with a prong made from a 16 penny nail, Fig. 7-B, and the other made from 3/16 inch copper ground wire that has been flattened into a wedge shape, Fig. 7-C. Wedge shaped and pointed copper tipped notching tools have become quite popular among modern knappers. Today very few knappers pressure flake and notch with antler.

Punches are used for indirect percussion. They are also made from antler tines of various sizes. The larger ones are the size of small diameter billets, Fig. 4-D, and are used for driving blades off cores. The punch that I now use has an antler sleeve and a point made from 1/4 inch copper ground wire, Fig. 7-E. These combo punches are very handy for heavy platform preparation and they also work quite well for indirect percussion as done on Danish daggers and axes. I also use a shortened 16 penny nail for punching out deep notches in certain Archaic type points. This may not be authentic because the same operation can be done by pressure, however, it saves a lot of wear and tear on my arm.

Abrading stones are made from quartzite or sandstone pebbles and are similar to hammerstones in shape and size. They are used for grinding the edge to prepare the striking platform. Some knappers, especially those who use copper billets, have gone to using broken carborundum wheels for abraders.

Until you become more adept at chipping you will need to wear something to protect your hands and eyes. If you choose to work on the leg you will have to make a pad of soft leather to protect it. Gloves should be worn, at least one on the hand that holds the flint. Your eyes can be protected from tiny splinters by wearing goggles, safety glasses or shooting glasses.

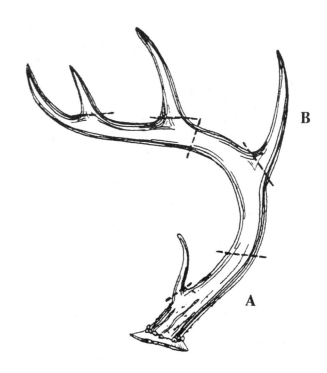

FIG. 6. *Cutting up a deer antler. A, the trunk becomes the large billet; tines, B, become pressure flakers. Racks can be held in a vise and dismembered with a hacksaw.*

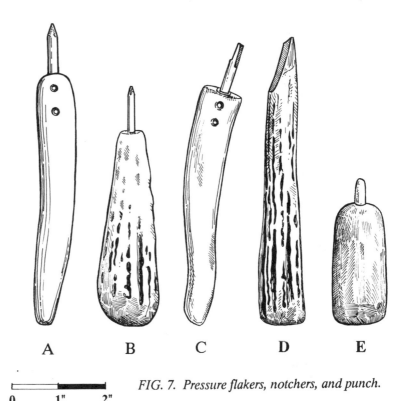

A   B   C   D   E

0   1"   2"

FIG. 7. *Pressure flakers, notchers, and punch.*

Chapter 4
THEORY AND TERMINOLOGY

Before we can begin our study of flint knapping in earnest, certain important terms and theories must be defined and discussed. Since this book is mostly about making bifaces, we will begin with a definition of this term and continue with other definitions that will be essential to your understanding of the craft. This will be followed by an in-depth discussion of flint knapping theory along with some suggestions on how to go about learning the art.

A **biface** is a flint tool, projectile point, or preform that has a simple edge and two faces worked by flaking. Good examples of complete bifaces are corner notch projectile points, commonly referred to as "arrowheads". Along with bifaces one finds cores, flakes, blades, and uniface tools. Together these comprise the flaked stone artifacts found in North America.

A **preform** is an unfinished biface that has been roughed out from either a spall struck from a core or made directly from a single piece of flint.

Cores are nodules or large blocks of raw stone from which spalls, flakes, and blades are struck. These flakes and blades may undergo slight modifications or **retouch** while being made into knives, burins, scrapers, or borers, or they may be further modified by bifacial or unifacial flaking. Cores for producing biface stock are fairly simple while blade cores can be quite complex. Both will be shown in detail in following chapters.

A **unifacial** tool or point is made from a spall, blade or flake by working one face only. Usually the dorsal face (see Fig. 8) is the one chosen for modification. At this point we must distinguish between a flake and a blade as well as define their attributes. I will also describe how they came to be, for each is a key to some portion of the knapping process.

Blades are struck from a prepared core and are at least twice as long as they are wide with near parallel or gradually tapering edges. Due to certain aspects of their geometry they are often referred to as **prismatic blades**. They should not be confused with **biface blades** which are large, bifacially worked, oval, leaf shaped or triangular points or knives that are usually unnotched.

Flakes comprise most of the debitage found on prehistoric sites. More may be found in association with quarries and workshops, and less in distant camps far from the source of raw material. **Spalls** are large flakes intended for use as blank stock for bifaces. They may be 3 to 6 inches in length or larger. Flakes and spalls are rounded or irregular in outline and are usually wider than blades. Except for length to width ratio, they pretty much share the same characteristics, Fig. 8.

FIG. 8. FLAKE TERMINOLOGY

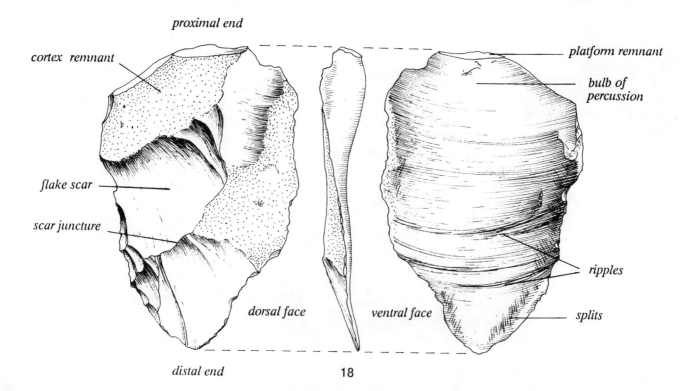

proximal end

cortex remnant

platform remnant

bulb of percussion

flake scar

scar juncture

ripples

splits

dorsal face

ventral face

distal end

Spalls, flakes, and blades like bifaces have a single edge or **margin** and two faces: a **dorsal face** or hump side and a **ventral face** or flat side. The dorsal face bears scars from previous flake removals or cortex from the outside of the nodule if it was one of the first to be struck. Such flakes are known as **dccortication flakes.** The ventral face will have a bulb of percussion, ripples, and splits characteristic of the side that faced the core or preform from which it was struck.

Near the **proximal** or upper end of the flake one will find the **bulb of percussion.** I believe this is formed by the sudden build-up of force as the **fracture front** is initiated. As the front advances, it ripples through the material like waves generated by a stone hitting a pool of water. Because flint is a solid, it breaks, and the record of that blow is frozen for all time. Bulbs and **ripples,** or **compression waves** or **rings,** as they are also referred to, are suppose to vary from **prominent** to **diffused.** This depends upon the amount of force used and the type and hardness of the percussor. These attributes are prominent for hammerstones and diffused for antler. However, there may be other factors causing such variations, so care must be taken when interpreting bulbs and ripples.

When a flake is struck a depression is left at the edge of the preform by the removal of the bulb. This is the **negative bulb.** The entire negative flake is referred to as a **flake scar** and the way these flakes are ordered is called a **flake scar pattern.** A master knapper can exercise considerable control over the size and orientation of the flakes, thus producing random, parallel, oblique and other patterns almost at will.

Ridges formed where the scars meet are called **scar junctures.** Along with humps and places of excessive thickness, they constitute the areas of high relief while troughs formed by negative scars form areas of low relief. The fact that fracture fronts have a tendency to follow junctures and other high spots is used to full advantage by the knapper. When you see him stop and study the piece he is working, he is checking the topography of the preform, looking for areas that need more flakes.

Some flakes, especially the thicker ones, will have **platform remnants** left above the bulbs. These are portions of **natural** or **prepared platforms** that stayed on the end of the flake when it was struck off. Prepared platforms are those areas along the edge that are purposely flattened or dulled by chipping and/or **abrading** so that the flakes come off cleanly when the edge is struck. If the edge is left sharp it will crush. If the platform is not prepared properly for the size, thickness and direction of the flake desired, flakes may terminate in a **hinge** or **step fracture** instead of feathering out cleanly, or they may not come off at all. Natural platforms are those that already exist and are in line with areas that the knapper wishes to work, so

he takes advantage of them with little or no modification. These occur more frequently in raw material processing and during the early stages of bifacing.

On a flake's ventral face one may notice fine, hairline cracks called **splits** which fan out from below the bulb of percussion across the surface at right angles to the ripples. They may also be found on scars. Under normal conditions splits are always present to a greater or lesser degree, depending upon the quality and grain size of the raw material. I believe that these are caused by slight bending of the preform when it is struck. The surface of the stone is stretched so that it splits. If the preform is bent too much by an improper blow, one of these splits will open up and the preform will fail.

As one's skill increases through practice he will be able to read the preform as he goes, choose the right tool for the job, prepare the edges properly, and meter his blows for maximum effect without fear of breakage. He will also learn how to hold the preform to dampen shock while lengthening the flakes and to hold the preform at the proper angle.

Holding positions and angles go hand in hand because the swing of the percussor remains basically the same while the preform is tilted to get the proper angle. Remember the BB and the glass? What is called the **Hertzian Cone** forms at about 100 degrees, Fig. 9, so the angle of force is 130 degrees to the plane of the fracture. In the past this angle was said to be measured from the **center plane,** which is an imaginary plane of reference that runs through the center of the biface from edge to edge. These measurements are incorrect. Drawings that were based on this concept were difficult to understand because the preform was always shown in a horizontal position with the center plane perfectly level and the arrows showing the force were moved about. In reality the arc of the percussor

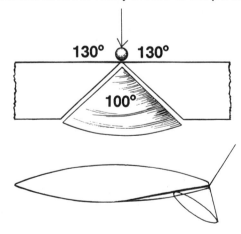

FIG. 9. *Above, cross section of a plate glass window with BB impact and Hertzian Cone. Below, the Hertzian Cone theory as it applies to flake removal from the edge of a preform.*

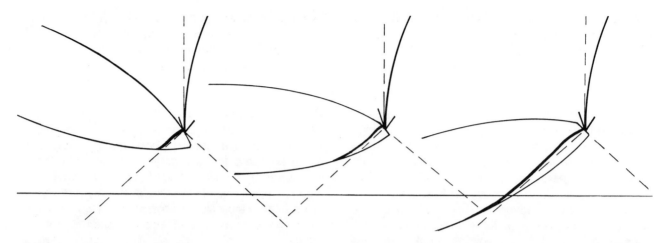

FIG. 10. Level line drawings showing tilt of preform for short, medium and long flakes. Dashed lines represent the theoretical Hertzian Cone and true angle of force application. Heavy curved arrows show the path of the percussor. Heavy, darkened lines through the cross-section of the preform represent the plane of fracture. (Many of the cross-section drawings in this book are of this type, while others shown in perspective or that show blows dealt to both edges are not.)

is the constant. The vertex of the angle is at the point of contact with the edge. The preform is tilted off level to get most of the longer flakes, leveled for short flakes, and slightly past level in the other direction, for the shortest flakes. Fig. 10 clearly shows this theory and this type of illustration is called a **level line drawing** because it uses an imaginary level line as a base for reference. Though correctly shown as an arc, the direction of force is always at 90 degrees to the level line when it contacts the edge. The Hertzian Cone has been added as a dashed line and the plane of the fracture, which is actually curved, is shown as a solid, darkened line. These drawings are easier for a beginner to understand because the first thing he learns is how to swing and strike. Since these two factors remain more or less constant, for the different lengths of flakes all that has to be done is match the angles shown in the illustrations. However, when all of the preceding factors are considered including the variable shape of the stone being worked, that is, no two are ever exactly alike, the situation becomes very complex. Enter the chaos theory as it applies to flint knapping.

Chaos means without form, confused, unorganized, and that is what enters the mind of a person who watches a master knapper for the first time, especially an individual who has some familiarity with stone tools but has never seen any made. What amazes them is the rapidity with which a formless rock takes shape as it is hammered by a multitude of what appears to be random blows. However, if the observer were to continue to watch the knapper for several weeks, definite patterns of working or **reduction strategies** would emerge, thus bringing some order to the chaos. In the past there have been many attempts to put these strategies and scenarios in some sort of comprehen-

sible order. As far as I'm concerned most of these (mine included) have not been as successful as they could have been. The problem is that flint knapping is not a true linear step by step craft: "Saw off A on dotted line and glue to B where indicated." It's more like: "Decide where next to take off flake A, prepare the platform by using short pressure strokes, grind, strike off A. A doesn't remove enough mass, prepare for B and C, that should do it. However, after B and C are gone, with that particular problem, the edge is so far out of alignment that a whole new series of flakes is needed to realign it." Meanwhile that envisioned 4 inch Dovetail is fast becoming a 3 inch Adena.

Because of these complexities a normal outline for thought processes concerning lithic reduction could not be achieved. What I ended up with was the multiple level flow chart shown in Fig. 11. It is based somewhat on a revised version of the lithic reduction continuum which progresses through the center of the diagram from raw material to finished product. The peripherals deal with factors and options, all of which have to be considered at the same time or at certain intervals during the reduction process. Study this carefully and pay close attention to all that goes on at any and every stage for the rest of the book is based on this chart.

The lithic reduction continuum as described by Callahan (Callahan 1979) and modified by the author is supposed to describe what happens to a biface as it is worked and is also used as a classification for unfinished pieces. The continuum is roughly divided into six "stages" and possibly a seventh. Because these stages are part of a continuum they are a bit arbitrary. In other words as the flakes are removed and the biface reduced, it sort of phases out of one stage and into another, Fig. 12.

FIG. 11

THOUGHT PROCESS FOR LITHIC REDUCTION CONTINUUM
(as applies to artifact series of North America)

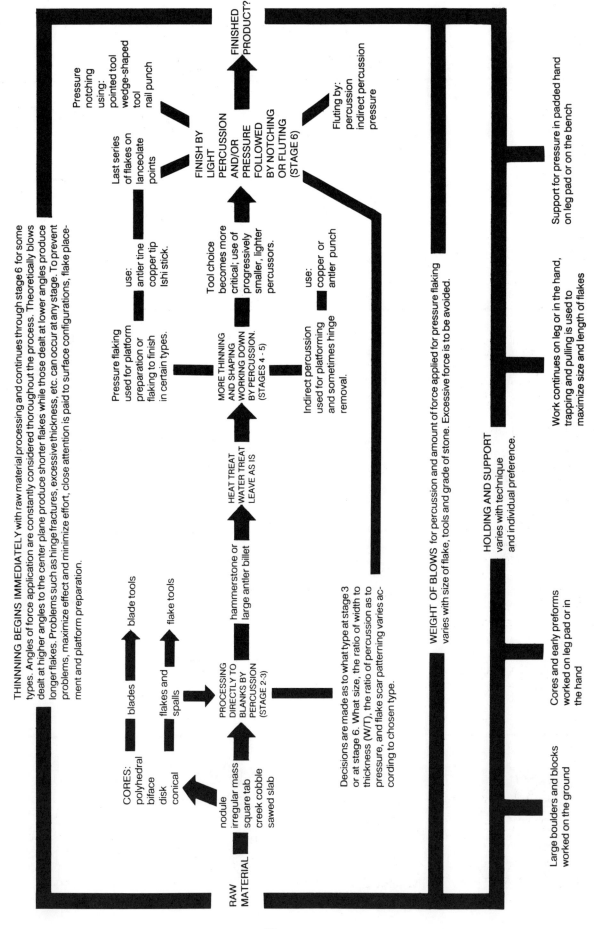

THINNNING BEGINS IMMEDIATELY with raw material processing and continues through stage 6 for some types. Angles of force application are constantly considered thoroughout the process. Theoretically blows dealt at higher angles to the center plane produce shorter flakes while those dealt at lower angles produce longer flakes. Problems such as hinge fractures, excessive thickness, etc. can occur at any stage. To prevent problems, maximize effect and minimize effort, close attention is paid to surface configurations, flake placement and platform preparation.

RAW MATERIAL

nodule
irregular mass
square tab
creek cobble
sawed slab

CORES:
polyhedral
biface
disk
conical

blades → blade tools

flakes and spalls → flake tools

PROCESSING DIRECTLY TO BLANKS BY PERCUSSION (STAGE 2-3)

hammerstone or large antler billet

Decisions are made as to what type at stage 3 or at stage 6. What size, the ratio of width to thickness (W/T), the ratio of percussion as to pressure, and flake scar patterning varies according to chosen type.

HEAT TREAT
WATER TREAT
LEAVE AS IS

MORE THINNING AND SHAPING WORKING DOWN BY PERCUSSION. (STAGES 4 - 5)

use:
antler tine
copper tip
Ishi stick.

Pressure flaking used for platform preparation or flaking to finish in certain types.

Tool choice becomes more critical; use of progressively smaller, lighter percussors.

Indirect percussion used for platforming and sometimes hinge removal.

use:
copper or antler punch

Last series of flakes on lanceolate points

FINISH BY LIGHT PERCUSSION AND/OR PRESSURE FOLLOWED BY NOTCHING OR FLUTING (STAGE 6)

Pressure notching using:
pointed tool
wedge-shaped tool
nail punch

Fluting by:
percussion
indirect percussion
pressure

FINISHED PRODUCT?

WEIGHT OF BLOWS for percussion and amount of force applied for pressure flaking varies with size of flake, tools and grade of stone. Excessive force is to be avoided.

HOLDING AND SUPPORT varies with technique and individual preference.

Large boulders and blocks worked on the ground

Cores and early preforms worked on leg pad or in the hand

Work continues on leg or in the hand, trapping and pulling is used to maximize size and length of flakes

Support for pressure in padded hand on leg pad or on the bench

21

FIG. 12. THE LTIHIC REDUCTION CONTINUUM

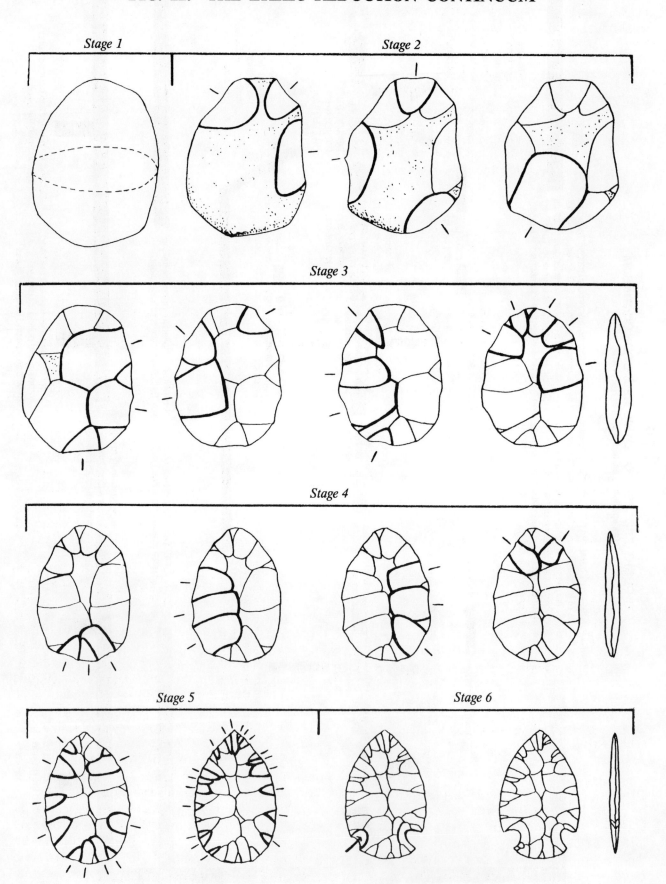

Stage 1   *Stage 2*

Stage 3

Stage 4

Stage 5   *Stage 6*

Stage 1, Obtaining Raw Materials: The raw materials come from either a single piece of flint, a small nodule, a spall from a nodule, or from a prepared core.

Stage 2, Edging: Remove round, square or thin sharp edges by flaking with the hammerstone and/or billet leaving a rough, wavy edge all the way around the blank. At this stage you will have a hand axe of sorts. At any time during the continuum the biface might be used as a tool. For example: a heavy quarry blank could be used as a chopper before becoming a knife or spear point.

Stage 3, Primary Thinning: The edge is straightened and the most prominent humps and ridges are removed. Here it is necessary to prepare and use striking platforms in order to extend the flakes to or slightly beyond the center of the piece.

Stage 4, Secondary Thinning: The edge is ground with the abrader or striking platforms are prepared below the center plane of the preform, whichever is necessary for the removal of more thinning flakes that extend well beyond the center line. They should considerably undercut previous scars so that the point becomes thin more rapidly than it becomes narrow. Also at this stage the piece starts to assume the desired shape. (The **center line** or median line is an imaginary line that is drawn across the face of the preform from tip to center of the base. This should not be confused with the center plane.)

Stage 5, Shaping: The edge is further straightened by light blows with the small antler and/or pressure flaking as the biface assumes the desired shape, triangular, leaf shaped or other.

Stage 6, Finishing: Here the preform is finished by notching, fluting, basal grinding, and minor retouching if necessary.

Stage 7, Reworking: Sometimes the continuum doesn't end with the finished product. Through use and wear a point or tool will get dull or be broken. In this case the piece is salvaged by reworking or resharpening. For example: a scraper or drill can be made from a broken point and a knife can be resharpened many times by beveling.

Along with the lithic reduction continuum is another standard that can be used to gauge a preform's progress. This is the **W/T ratio** or the ratio of width to thickness, Fig. 13. In simple terms, if a point is three inches wide and one inch thick it has a W/T ratio of three to one. The average stage 2 biface is over 3/1, stage 3 is under 3/1, stage 4 is about 4/1, and the

FIG. 13. WIDTH/THICKNESS RATIOS
after Callahan (1979:18)

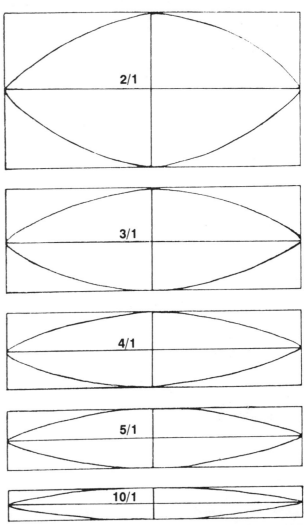

average completed artifact, depending upon the type, is from 4/1 to 6/1. However, certain lanceolate points with prominent median ridges may be 3/1, and large, broad bifaces such as Snyders points or Texas base tang knives will go 10/1 or thinner.

One of the major problems with the stage theory as described and illustrated above is that a rounded cobble or nodule is shown as the starting piece. No spalls or single, odd-shaped pieces are mentioned. In the early stages strategies for dealing with them differ. Only by stage 3 are all preforms pretty much standardized. Today master knappers begin thinning immediately, especially on those odd pieces, taking advantage of natural platforms that most of them will conveniently have. There are two good reasons for this departure. One, edging is a costly stage that is unnecessary if you are fully familiar with all of the edge preparation and mass removal scenarios that will be thoroughly covered in the next chapter. There is no reason why those longer, thinning flakes can't be driven off from the very beginning. Secondly, perhaps 60% or more of all the raw material available in the midwestern United States comes in odd pieces with a mixture of square, rounded and/or sharp edges. So, the would-be knapper is forced to deal with them whether he likes it or not.

Actually, the continuum, as it works out for me is a three stage process. The first stage is raw material processing where the stone is found, quarried, broken down, and roughed out into irregular preforms ready for transport home. This operation has come to be called **spalling out**. Stage 2 is further thinning and shaping until it reaches the equivalent of Callahan's Stage 5, (Callahan 1979:11). Early in this stage or right after spalling, heat treatment is considered. Stage 3 sees the piece finished by notching or fluting and some minor pressure retouch if necessary. There is no equivalent to Stage 7 as most points end up behind glass in display cases.

How does one go about learning such a complex skill as flint knapping?

To date there have been several courses or learning strategies proposed. One of the most complex is the **phase system** as set down by Callahan, (Callahan 1979:37-38). The phases are:

Learning Phase A - circumferential edging so as to create edge-angles of between 55 to 75 degrees, but so that were reduction to continue with the same strategy, the biface would become narrow at a more rapid rate than it would become thin. (**Edge angles** are measured from face to face through the mass of the preform. The vertex is at the edge.)

Learning Phase B - flaking to the median line so as to cover the entire surface of the biface with flake scars. This creates edge angles of between rougly 40 to 60 degrees, a width/thickness ratio of between roughly 3/1 and 4/1, and a lenticular cross-section. Were reduction to continue with the same strategy, the biface would become narrow at about the same rate as it would become thin.

Learning Phase C - flaking to and beyond the median line so as to create edge angles of between roughly 25 to 45 degrees, a width/thickness ratio in excess of about 4/1, and a flattened cross-section. Were reduction to continue with the same strategy, the biface would become thin at a more rapid rate than it would become narrow.

Learning Phase D - flaking to create a near parallel-sided biface with the attributes of Phase C.

Learning Phase E - flaking to create a biface with the attributes of Phase D while arriving at a predeter-

mined shape, mass, lateral edge alignment, and equal working of each face at the same time.

Learning Phase F - flaking to create a biface with the attributes of Phase E and with predetermined flake removal sequences and/or other specific surface attributes.

These phases follow the evolution of lithic technology. With some instruction, most people are able to master Phases A and B in a reasonably short time, a day or two. Phase C could take a month or much longer as a person learns to handle the antler billet and to prepare the edge so that flakes can be driven past the median to accomplish rapid thinning. After Phase C is mastered, D and E may quickly follow with persistence. After two to three years many beginners have become serious flint workers and can turn out some nice small to medium sized points. However, they are still unable to completely control the process to produce at will an exact replica of any given type.

Even some commercial knappers seem to be unaware of the fact that each artifact type has its own set of "specs" as I call them, or **attributes**, as they are referred to in the literature. These attributes are used to define one type from another. They include: proper size and shape, (as seen in silhouette or outline), proper width to thickness ratios, correct scar patterns, presence or absence of serrations and/or beveling, being made of the correct material, and having the proper basal treatment such as notching and/or fluting and basal grinding. Those who understand all of the above and can act accordingly have entered the last phase and are well on their way to becoming masters. A master can easily reproduce all or most of the types in his area. However, he may still remain a student at the Phase F level if he chooses to continue his education by learning to reproduce other types from outside his state or even his country.

After teaching many weekend flint knapping courses and taking on numerous single students, I have found that the phase system is hard to teach in such a short time. Because of its complexity, I would have to work with a single student on a daily basis for several months. The reason flint knapping is taught that way in colleges is that most of the students are training to be anthropologists and archaeologists and not part time or professional flint knappers. They are taught the science of lithic technology, not the art of flint knapping. Since this book was written to include both areas we must look at the alternatives.

Many self-taught knappers I know first learned to work flint by making small arrow points from chips left by other knappers, from bottle glass, or from thin-sawn slabs of obsidian, Fig. 14. By taking a small, thin chip and edging it by scraping and/or beveling, and then pressure flaking a bird point, one can get the feel for the proper angles as well as a feel for the tools. With only a few hours of instruction the student can be hard at work making points one after the other. This gives the beginner training and confidence for the next step, obtaining his own flakes by working a core with a hammerstone and antler billet. Making cores is an excellent introduction to percussion flaking. By striking off flakes and blades the beginner will learn how to gauge his blows and handle his tools in preparation for edging and thinning some of the thicker flakes.

The above is what we call the **birdpoint method.** However, there is a third strategy called the **preform first method.** This is where the student or beginner is shown how to edge river cobbles in preparation for heat treating, and how to break up large blocks and nodules to make rough hand axe-like preforms or quarry blanks. He then saves the larger and/or thicker ones and proceeds to learn percussion with the billet and pressure flaking on the smaller and thinner ones. As his skill and knowledge improves he then goes back to his stash for the bigger, harder to work pieces. This method works best for those in flint-rich areas while the birdpoint method would better suit those who have limited resources.

FIG. 14. MAKING SMALL ARROW POINTS

A. Flake selection. *Select flakes that are thin, flat, straight and triangular in shape. If flint is not available then use triangular shards of window or bottle glass. On the flakes the bulb end will be the point. As skill improves less perfect flakes can be modified and used.*

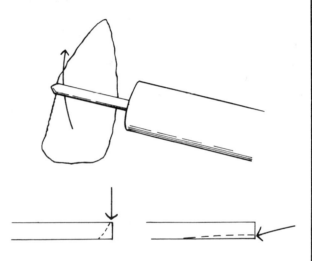

B. Edging. *Edging for sharp flakes is done by scraping with the side of the pressure tool with a lateral and downward stroke. This is to strengthen the edge and for platform preparation. Square edged pieces of glass can be edged by beveling with straight, downward strokes. It is also possible to push long flakes off the square edge but hinging is more likely if exact, proper angle is not used.*

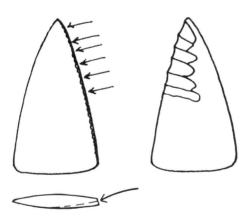

C. Thinning and shaping. *After lightly abrading the platforms the first set of thinning flakes can be removed by smooth, inward, and downward strokes at the angles shown. To shape and finish the point several series of flakes may have to be removed. Platform preparation and grinding is used when necessary so longer flakes will come off clean.*

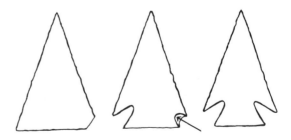

D. Notching. *The point is finished by notching. To make notching easier you might wish to remove the corners for a corner notch point. This helps to prevent breakage of the ears. (For more on notching see Chapters 6 and 9).*

Chapter 5
REDUCTION STRATEGIES

This chapter will deal with biface reduction strategies and scenarios from spalling-out to Stage 5. The focus will be on percussion flaking techniques with some mention of indirect percussion and pressure as they apply to platform preparation. Each figure and accompanying text covers a certain strategy or scenario; as the work progresses they will be encountered, either singly or in combination. At this point, no problems other than those of straightforward reduction will be discussed. Obviously, the beginner will not be able to follow these instructions without encountering some serious technical difficulties. These will be dealt with in Chapter 7. For now everything will move along as if the reader is watching a demonstration put on by a master knapper.

Raw material processing begins with the breaking down of nodules and blocks into spalls and angular pieces. Afterward some primary thinning of the thickest areas is done in preparation for heat treating and/or transport and storage.

The first and worst case scenario is the solid, round nodule. Fortunately, in the natural environment these are rare. Most have already been halved or quartered by freezing and thawing. A higher percentage of them may be found when limestone is being freshly quarried (those that have survived blasting) or in the residual of younger formations in warmer climates like in Texas. Also, the survival rate will be higher for tougher, grainier stones, as opposed to slicker ones. There seems to be a lot more small nodules, those below 4 inches, that have made it through the eons in one piece. If a nodule is less than 3 inches in diameter it's not worth the trouble, unless that is all you have and the stone is of high quality.

The most common problem that occurs when one is trying to split a round nodule is **coneing.** This happens when the angle is wrong or the blow is too light and a cone forms inside the nodule below the point of impact, Fig. 15. The force applied must be substantial enough to penetrate the cortex and shear the nodule. If the angle of the blow comes in at about 20 degrees off perpendicular, one half of the nodule should pull away from the other. Fig. 16 shows what happens as the fracture changes direction and the stone separates. (Actually, what occurs here is the conversion of the cone into a **planer crack split**). This is the best approach if the nodule doesn't roll around too much. The way to prevent this is to cradle it in a hollow in the ground.

Even though the nodule is halved, a portion of the cone may still remain intact along with other un-

desirable cracks that were formed during impact. This area should be trimmed away back to solid material before further spalling or preforming.

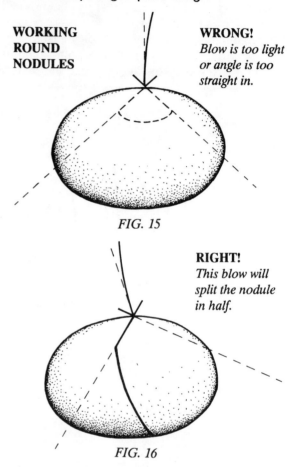

WORKING ROUND NODULES

WRONG!
Blow is too light or angle is too straight in.

FIG. 15

RIGHT!
This blow will split the nodule in half.

FIG. 16

There is another type of whole nodule that is shaped somewhat like a flying saucer. It has a rim around it which makes a nice, natural platform. Just strike at 90 degrees to the plane of the rim and above the edge for the first spall, Fig. 17. If struck 20 to 30 degrees or so off perpendicular the stone can be split almost in half, Fig. 18. This works best for those that are 8 inches in diameter or less, because they can be supported on the leg, where it is easier to control the angle of the strike by tilting the nodule. Besides, most knappers prefer to split the small nodules and make one fairly large preform out of each half.

Fig. 19 shows the author working on a 40 lb. Texas nodule lying on the ground. Such nodules are too large to be handled on the leg safely. Blocks and smaller nodules of 15 lbs. or less are worked with greater accuracy while being supported on the leg. A thick leather pad is used to protect the knee, Fig. 20.

WORKING SAUCER SHAPED NODULES

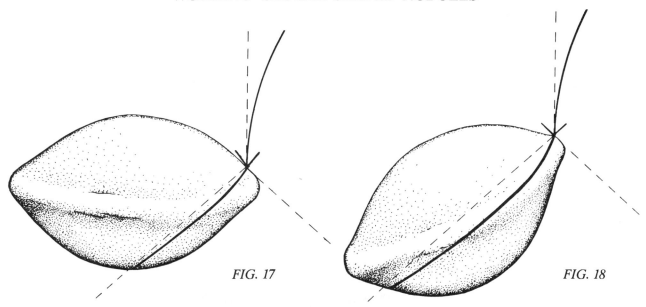

FIG. 17

FIG. 18

HOLDING POSITIONS FOR NODULES AND BLOCKS

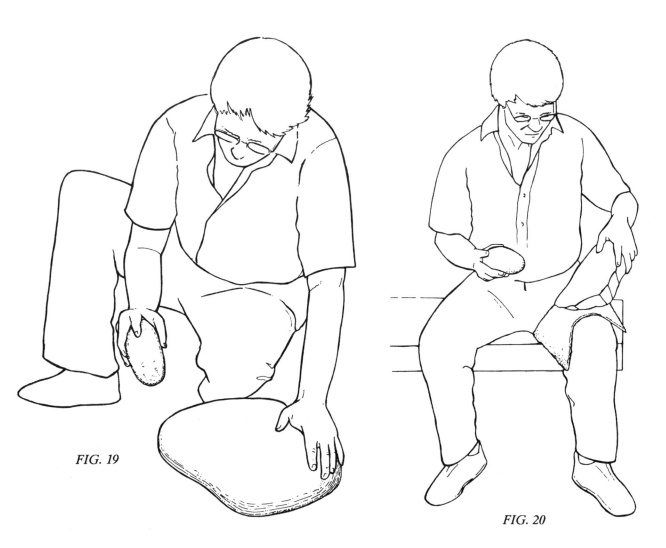

FIG. 19

FIG. 20

FIG. 21. WORKING A NODULE INTO A BIFACE CORE

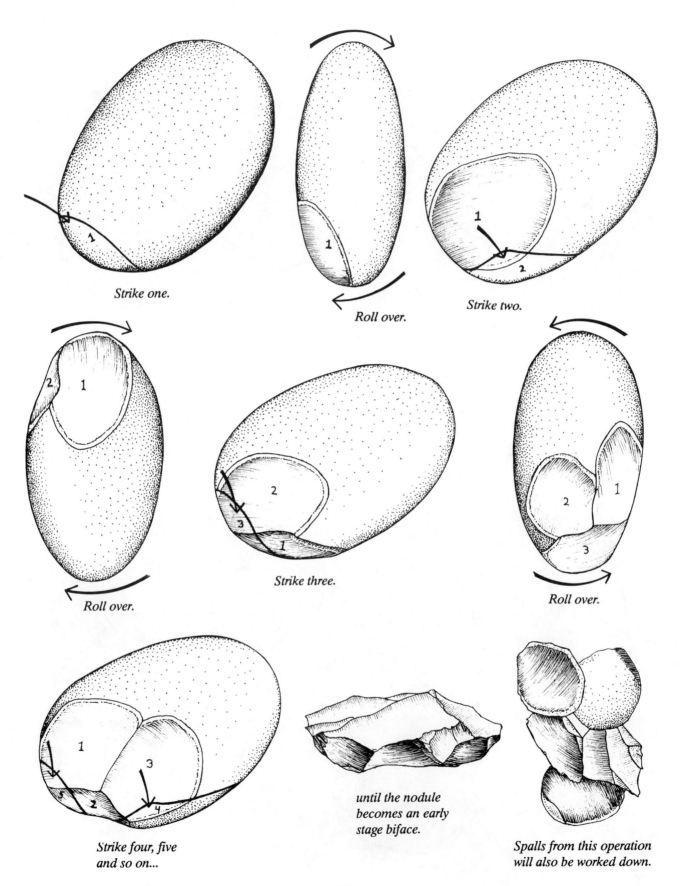

Strike one.

Roll over.

Strike two.

Roll over.

Strike three.

Roll over.

Strike four, five and so on...

until the nodule becomes an early stage biface.

Spalls from this operation will also be worked down.

Now for the big one on the ground, the scar left by the spall you have removed from the rim will be the platform for the next strike or two. When those spalls are removed the nodule is once again turned over and more blows are dealt to the flats left behind, Fig. 21. This zig-zagging around and into the stone is continued until a disk of sorts is all that is left of the center. This type of core is called a **biface core** because it is worked all around the edge bifacially until the center becomes too small to be profitable. Then it too can be turned into a preform. I will sometimes work a monster nodule like this for the biggest preform I can get out of its center. In this case the spalls are secondary. This is called **center cutting** and if you don't know what you're doing it can be quite wasteful. If the nodule is solid it is better to have it sawed into several one inch thick slabs.

Half nodules are worked by striking spalls off the rounded sides using the flat as a platform, Fig. 22. The angles may vary between 20 and 40 degrees off perpendicular to the flat, depending upon the curvature of the sides and how large a spall you want. Also, the placement of the impact point will be closer to the edge for shorter, thinner pieces, Fig. 22-A, and farther in for larger, thicker ones, Fig. 22-B. This works to a point where the bulb attempts to become a cone because there is too much mass between the impact point and the edge.

Large half nodules will yield a number of spalls from 3 to 8 inches, Fig. 22-C. Smaller ones are best broken into three pieces, two sides and a center, Fig. 22-D.

FIG. 22. WORKING HALF NODULES

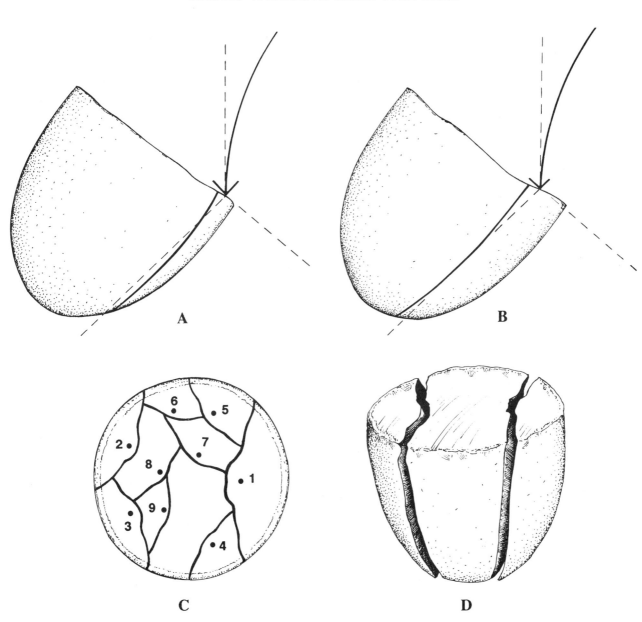

A

B

C

D

29

Quarter nodules, due to their shape, usually yield only one biface. In order to get a blank out of the one shown in Fig. 23-A, the interior edge is removed by driving several long flakes from one or both ends. Due to problems with the cortex, strike and angle miscalculations may cause hinging, Fig. 22-B, and overshooting, Fig. 22-C. To prevent this platforms are prepared by the removal of several flakes off the ends, Fig. 22-D, so a series of controlled long flakes can be run, Fig. 22-E and 22-F. Now the piece can be further thinned by taking off a number of decortiication flakes using the slanted sides as natural platforms, if they are at the proper angle, Fig. 22-G. Also on a second and/or third series of flakes removed from the edges, abrading may be necessary if the edge is too sharp or overhung.

FIG. 23. WORKING A QUARTER NODULE

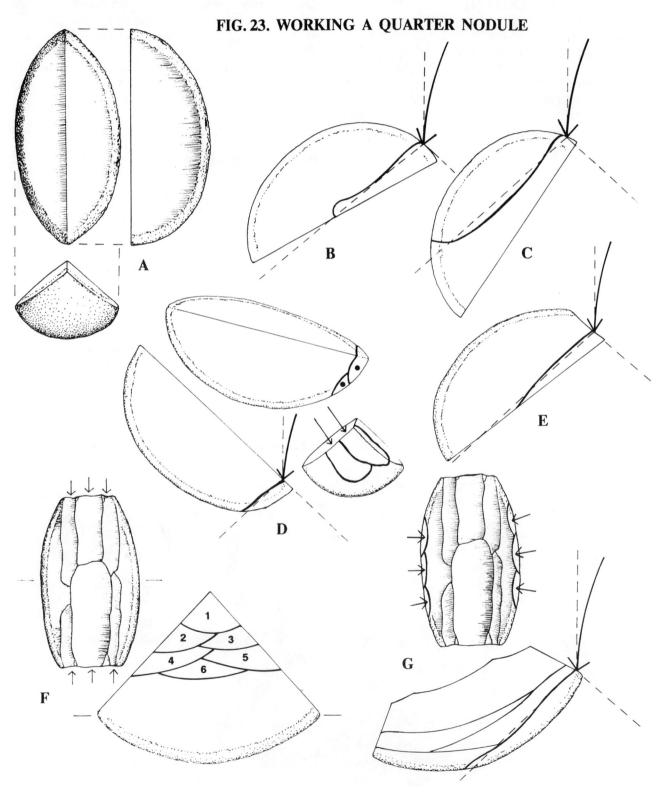

30

FIG. 24. ELONGATED NODULES

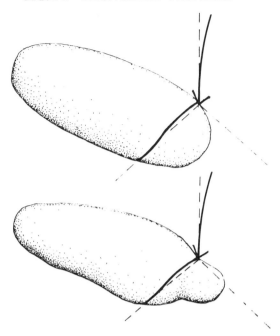

Nodules that are elongated or that have protrusions can be struck on the smaller end or one of the projections can be knocked off to gain access, Fig. 24.

Large blocks, boulders, and irregular pieces will present the knapper with numerous natural platforms as well as weather cracks that can be utilized. A mass of flint should be examined carefully for fractures. If cracks are found the stone can be gently thumped apart with the large hammerstone. I prefer to use a hammerstone instead of a sledge hammer for all but shearing round nodules because the impact is less harsh and spalls are not split as often. If the block is found to be solid, blows are dealt to flat areas depending upon the length and thickness of spalls desired, Fig. 25. This is basically the same procedure as used on half nodules.

FIG. 25. WORKING A BLOCK

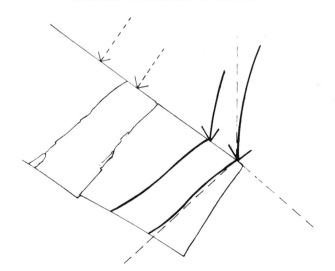

After the first spalls are struck it may be necessary to trim back the overhangs left by negative bulbs in preparation for the next series. These overhanging areas will distort your view of the solid mass below, thus causing you to strike too close to the true edge. Such mis-strikes end in too thin or too short a spall, Fig. 26. (This rule applies to nodules, odd pieces, and cores as well.)

FIG. 26. EDGE TRIMMING

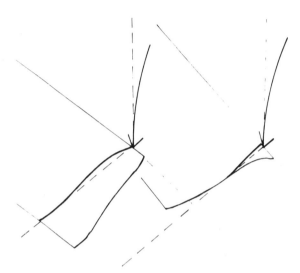

In actuality, perfectly flat surfaces like those shown above are not the norm for flint found in the field. Most surfaces that appear flat are slightly convex or concave. Naturally fractured blocks may have a negative scar as one of the "flat" surfaces. When using a concave surface as a platform, the angle of the blows must be leaned inward a few degrees in order to get the same spall as you would have gotten had you struck a flat surface, Fig. 27.

FIG. 27. CONCAVE SURFACE

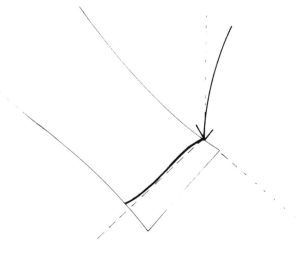

Convex surfaces like those that appear on some weather fractured nodules and the positive halves of those broken deliberately are a problem. If the bulge is too prominent the tool will skid off with little effect. In this case the frustrated amateur usually increases the amplitude of the blow to such an extent that the impact site is coned or the piece is sheared in an undesirable manner. To avoid this problem the convexity is worked off by flaking from the edge as shown in Fig. 28. This turns the convex surface into a concavity that is easily worked by the methods described earlier.

FIG. 28. CONVEX SURFACE

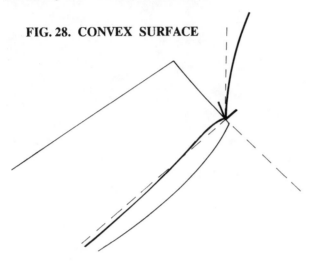

Another problem on blocks and boulders are sharp corners. These are knocked off as shown in Fig. 29-A The spalls that follow should be flatter and less angular, Fig. 29-B.

FIG. 29. WORKING OFF SHARP EDGES

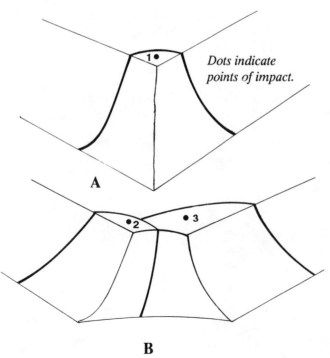

Dots indicate points of impact.

Those pieces that came off the corners are called ridged spalls, due to the sharp ridge running up their dorsal face. These shapes may also occur as weather fractures along with tabular pieces and square blocks. A fourth class of pre-preforms is made up of domed spalls, those that have a flat side and a humped side.

The procedure for working **ridged spalls**, Fig. 30, is similar to working quarter nodules. Trimming of the edge and some platform preparation may be necessary, Fig. 30-A. Then flakes are driven off from the proximal end (bulb end or thickest end) down the ridge, Fig. 30-B.

FIG. 30. WORKING RIDGED SPALLS

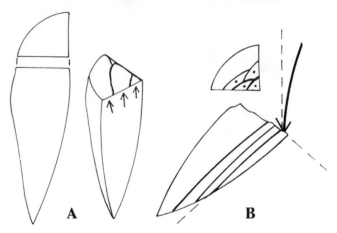

Square blocks and thick rectangular pieces are reduced by fracturing off opposing edges from the corners, Fig. 31-A. The edges that remain are used as platforms for lateral thinning flakes, 31-B.

FIG. 31. SQUARE BLOCKS

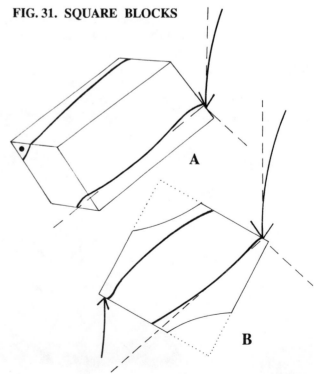

Tabular pieces are most often longer than they are wide and at least three times wider than they are thick. Shatter from cracked boulders, creek cobbles, and sawed slabs fall into this category. The problem here is changing a roughly rectangular cross-section into a more amenable, lenticular one. This problem can be solved in either of two ways: the first is what I call the **alternate flaking technique.** Here a wavy edge is worked down the long sides of the tab by alternate blows from face to face with each flake making a platform for its successor, Fig. 32-A, B, and C. With the wavy edge complete, Fig. 32-D, lateral thinning flakes are then struck off at the scar junctures, Fig. 32-F. Some platform preparation by pressure flaking and/or grinding will be necessary at the edge where the junctures form an angle, Fig. 32-E.

The **platform reversal technique** is the other way. Here the edges are beveled parallel one another to form a continuous platform, regardless of which way the short sides are leaning, Fig. 33-A. The next step is to run thinning flakes off the bevels, these usually terminate near the center line of the piece. The placement and angle of the blows are carefully controlled to prevent hinging, Fig. 33-B. In step three, a reversed platform is prepared by pressure flaking and/or punch flaking at a high angle, Fig. 33-C. Now another series of thinning flakes are struck. These will go in and meet or come close to those removed previously, Fig. 33-D. At the end of this operation you should have a biface with a centered edge that can be worked just like any other. The third series of flakes will further thin the piece and should get rid of what's left of the remaining flat surfaces, Fig. 33-E. On tabs wider than three inches, additional series of flakes may be needed. In this case the edges may become too thin and sharp and may need trimming back to make stronger platforms.

FIG. 32. ALTERNATE FLAKING OF TABULAR PIECES.

FIG. 33. PLATFORM REVERSAL TECHNIQUE

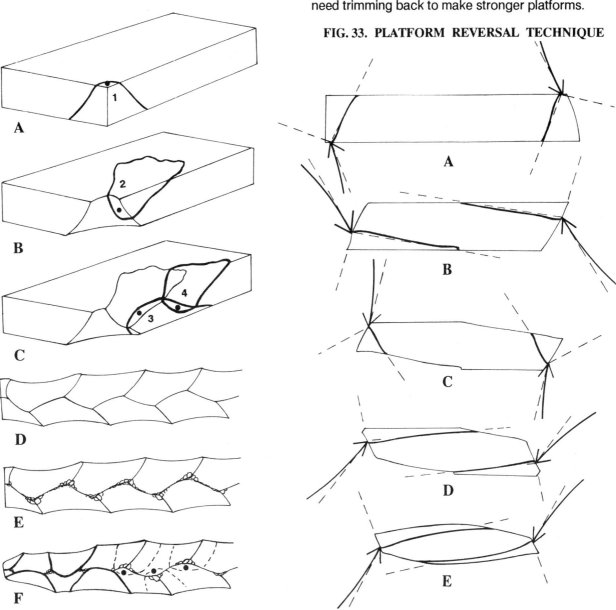

The easiest to work into preforms are large **domed spalls**. A continuous platform is beveled to the flat side, Fig. 34-A. Then the edge is abraded and the piece is turned over and the humped side is worked, removing the cortex and other areas of high relief, Fig. 34-B. Again, it may take more than one series of flake removals to thin these and edge preparation will have to be done for each group of flakes.

FIG. 34. DOMED SPALLS

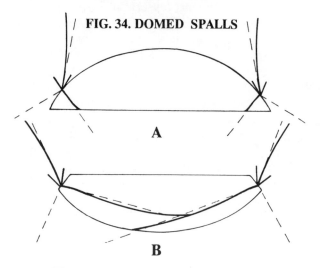

A

B

Now that we have a pile of early stage preforms ranging in size from 2 to 8 inches, we must decide what to do with them. If you are a beginner with little or no experience you should stay with the smaller and thinner pieces until you have mastered the basics well enough to produce a simple stemmed or corner notched point. It should be in the 2 to 3 inch range and have a centered edge and a W/T ratio of 5/1. For the master knapper this is no big deal. He has in mind what he wants, sees it in the stone, and, like a sculptor removes everything that doesn't look like the intended point. To do this, he controls the process of thinning, shaping, and centering the edge. The problem with middle stage bifaces is that all of this seems to happen at once. For a better understanding of the effect each of the above factors has on our preform let's consider them separately.

One could take a flake or spall and beat around on the edges until it was roughly the shape of an arrowhead. Though it resembles a projectile point in outline, it will not have a very good edge, nor will the cross-section be satisfactory unless it was made from an already thin piece of flint. You see these edged flakes for sale in tourist traps at fifty cents each. Surely we can do better than this!

If a chunk of stone was worked with a straight edge in mind, this could be achieved by removing flakes wherever there was a curve in the edge in an attempt to center it. In this case the edge may be straight while the preform is lopsided in outline or worse yet, too thick in cross-section with high edge angles, (not very effi-

cient for cutting or penetrating). Such points you may find in the east and south made by hammerstone percussion on less than desirable materials. The Indians did the best they could with what they had.

Now if one were to concentrate on thinning, he would end up with a biface that had a flattened lenticular cross-section. Even though its outline may be somewhat eccentric and the edges a bit wavy it would be thin and both faces would be covered with flake scars. All that has to be done to it to bring it into Stage 5 is a little more work to straighten the edge and while this is being done the piece is shaped. So you can see why so much emphasis is placed on thinning.

In order to properly thin a piece the first flakes must be made to remove high spots and excessive thickness. When both faces are leveled the edge will begin to straighten out. As more flakes are struck randomly or in series, the biface is worked equally on both faces to maintain an even contour and a centered edge. On domed or ridged preforms more may need to be removed from a face that is still too high. To facilitate such controlled work you must be able to predict with reasonable accuracy what length, shape, and thickness of flake is needed to do the job. Then prepare the platform, choose the tool, and deal the blow in the right place, at the right angle, and at the proper amplitude. Holding and support may become critical factors on longer, wider bifaces.

As a general rule for thinning, flakes are made to go past the center of the preform with a few almost reaching the opposite edge. The amount of material you wish to remove with a single flake is calculated with surface configuration and risk factors in mind. Flawed executions and outright destruction of the piece are ever present dangers. However, there are ways to lessen the risk.

A much safer approach would be a series of smaller flakes that peck away at the problem, but even this has a down side. More flake removals means more edge preparations and this translates into loss of size. If the novice knapper pays close attention to what happens when he is chipping and if he takes note of good and bad flakes and what he did to cause them he will quickly learn what he can get away with and what he can't.

Flake scar patterns can be controlled to a considerable degree in the later stages of production. For our project the flaking will be random percussion with pressure retouch, typical of the Archaic and Woodland periods. Though flakes may vary in size and orientation, what we are after is a nicely thinned point with a smooth surface. However, on larger points from these periods the patterns may be quite regular. This happens when a big preform is thinned and leveled early on and close attention is paid to spacing of flakes in the later stages. As we continue in the following chapters more will be said about patterning. For now we have to learn more about edge preparation and striking or we will never be able to get the flakes we need.

Of all the things we have to deal with in the reduction sequence, preparation of the edge is the most critical. If the platform is prepared properly the flake will come off with relative ease. A good platform will also make the edge more forgiving of mis-strikes and angle mis-calculations. There are two types of prepared platforms: continuous and isolated. Natural platforms can mimic both of these but are only used when they are in proper alignment for the desired flake. If not, they are reworked or removed altogether.

Continuous platforms are designed for the removal of more than one flake. Short sections of the edge may be prepared for a series aimed at a hump, or the entire margin from end to end may be beveled like we did for Fig. 33 and 34. These platforms may be 1/4 to 1/8 inch wide for heavy percussion to 1/16 inch or less for light percussion and pressure. They are made by a series of direct percussion or punch flakes for heavy platforms and pressure flaking and/or abrading for the lesser ones. Abrading alone may be enough for light percussion with the small billet and for most pressure work.

FIG. 35. CONTINUOUS PLATFORM

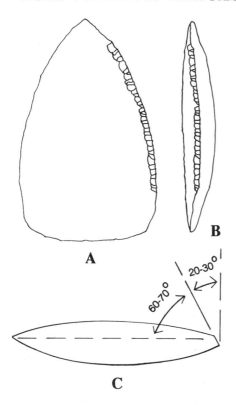

Fig. 35-A (obverse face) shows beveling flakes for a continuous platform. Fig. 35-B shows an edge that has been moved below the center plane by beveling flakes. In all platform preparations the beveling is done on the opposite face thus moving the edge closer to the face that is to be worked. Fig. 35-C shows the angle of the platform in relation to the center plane and perpendicular. Ideal platforms vary from 20 to 30 degrees off perpendicular or 60 to 70 degrees from center plane. (Note: antler billets, due to their tendency to throw longer flakes, are not the best tools for all platform beveling. A small hammerstone is better. However, I use the punch for almost all of my heavy percussion platforms, while I scrape the edge with the side of my pressure flaker or use the carborundum for lesser platforms.)

FIG. 36. SERIES FLAKING OFF CONTINUOUS PLATFORM

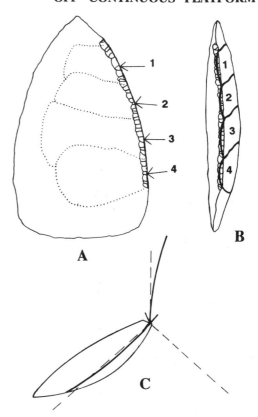

Fig. 36-A shows a series of flakes that have been removed to get at an area of excessive thickness on the reverse face. Fig. 36-B shows where the flakes came off the edge. Notice the order in which the flakes were struck. In this case the preform was held in a position with the tip pointing away from the knapper. For the best results at eating away thick areas the flakes should be run on a slight oblique angle working into the mass in a direction towards the knapper. Fig. 36-C shows the correct angle of the preform and angle of blows for maximum effect.

Isolated platforms are usually prepared on the edge where scar junctures meet the margin. This is done by whittling a slight concavity in the edge just above and below the juncture, after which the area is abraded. In

FIG. 37. WORKING ISOLATED PLATFORMS

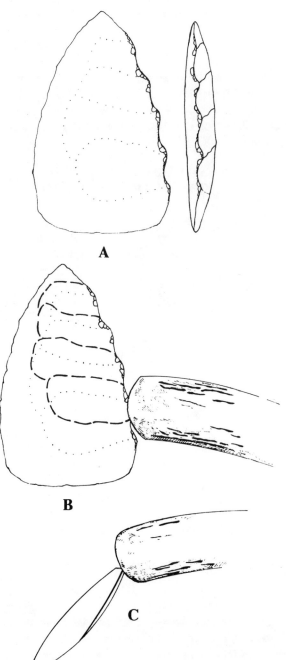

A

B

C

Fig. 37-A, this has been done on the obverse face. The light dotted lines show the junctures of existing flakes on the reverse face. Fig. 37-B shows flakes coming off the reverse face indicated by the heavy dashed lines. Note that the end of the billet only contacts the tip of the platform while clearing the rest of the edge. This allows for unobstructed power transmission with great control. Fig. 37-C shows the isolated platform that has been prepared just below the center plane. Because contact is isolated, striking angles can be a bit lower contributing to flake length.

Theoretically, blows dealt at higher angles to the center plane will produce shorter flakes, Fig. 38-A and B, and those at lower angles will produce longer flakes, Fig. 38-C and D, until the point of edge crushing, hinging, and/or overshooting is reached. However, because the path of the percussor is an arc the knapper perceives these angles to be lower than they actually are, except in the case of punch flaking. In order to further prevent breakage, longer flakes are usually struck from a point lower on the platform. Fig. 38 was designed to show the angles relative to one another and to alert the novice to a danger zone that exists where the angles are too low. If problems begin to occur then you will have to strike at a higher angle. Since this is not a level line drawing, you will have to tilt the book to check your holding positions.

As for tool choice and weight of blows: larger and heavier percussors for larger pieces and larger flakes, and smaller tools for smaller work. Force application will vary with size of flake and size of the tool. Also, less force will be used if platforms are properly prepared. The exceptions to this general rule are the use of smaller antler billets for heat treated materials and on very large bifaces, when they become very thin. I use antler for 90% of my work, even heavy preforming of raw stone before heat treating. A big moose billet seems to give me more control and flatter, larger flakes, thus aiding the thinning process early on. The

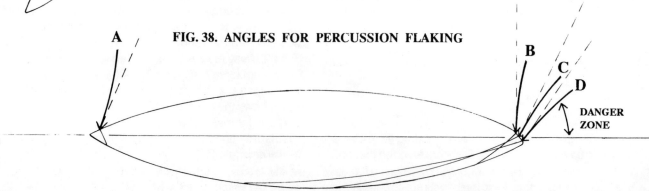

A   **FIG. 38. ANGLES FOR PERCUSSION FLAKING**   **B**   **C**   **D**   **DANGER ZONE**

choice is up to you. Once you have gained some experience in metering your blows, you will know when you are striking too hard. If the flake does not release on the second attempt the platform should be checked.

There are two basic holding-support techniques: freehand and anvil. In the **free hand technique** the piece is held in the left hand and the hammerstone or billet in the right. When the flakes come off they are caught by the fingers, released, and fall harmlessly to the ground. At first one may wish to wear a pair of gloves while using this technique. This method is widely practiced by a great many knappers who like the control, but are not bothered by the fear of injuries.

For those who are interested in both results and safety the **anvil technique** is the alternative. In a forge the hot iron is drawn from a fire and laid on an anvil where it is beaten to shape. In chipping the flint is also laid on an anvil. In this case the padded upper leg of the knapper supplies the support while the chips are caught between the pad and the preform. After a couple of blows you just shake the chips off the pad and go on working. This is the method that I use and when mastered it works just as well as the the freehand method. Fig. 38-46 clearly show several holding and support techniques. It is up to the individual to experiment and find those that best suit his style and physique.

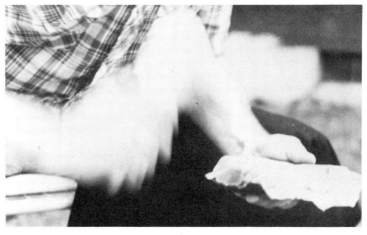

A

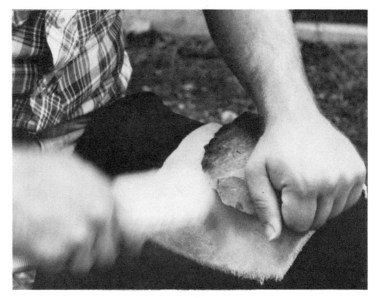

B

FIG. 38. These photos show the swing, (A) contact (B) and follow through (C) as well as three holding positions used in supporting a large preform.

The preform is held just tight enough to secure it. The swing of the large moose antler is slower and more arc-like, while smaller billets, moving at higher speed, are snapped against the edge like a whip. This motion requires a loose hold and more wrist action.

Most amateurs have trouble at first because they are unable to loosen up. They hold the billet too tight and do not rotate the wrist as the arm swings downward. This motion can be seen in the photos.

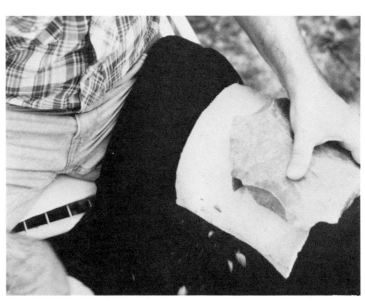

C

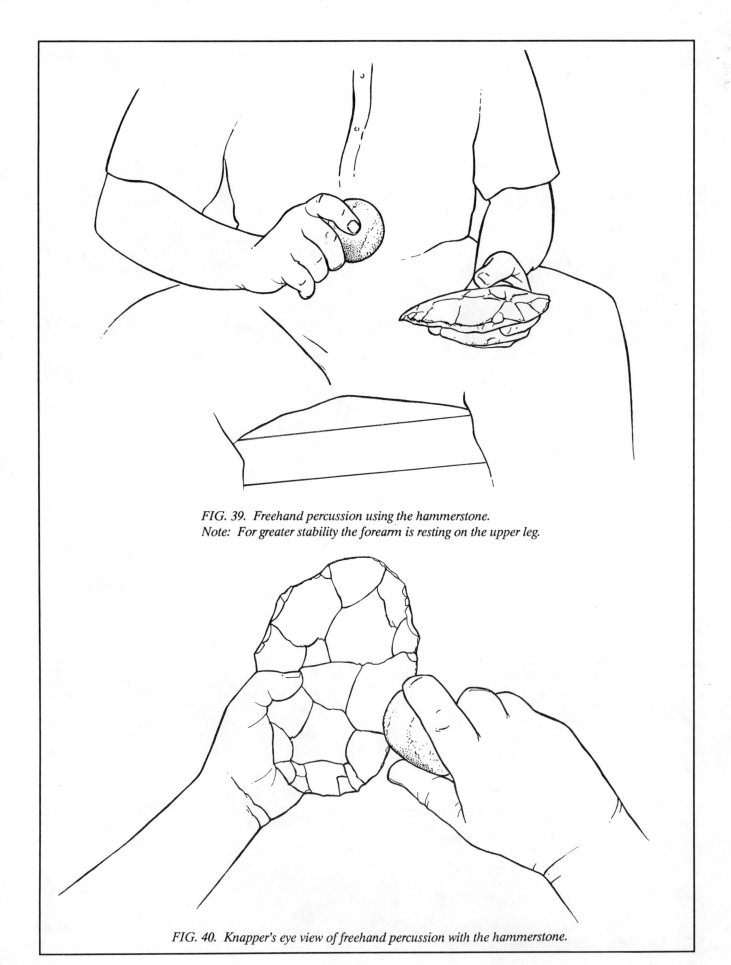

FIG. 39. *Freehand percussion using the hammerstone.*
Note: For greater stability the forearm is resting on the upper leg.

FIG. 40. *Knapper's eye view of freehand percussion with the hammerstone.*

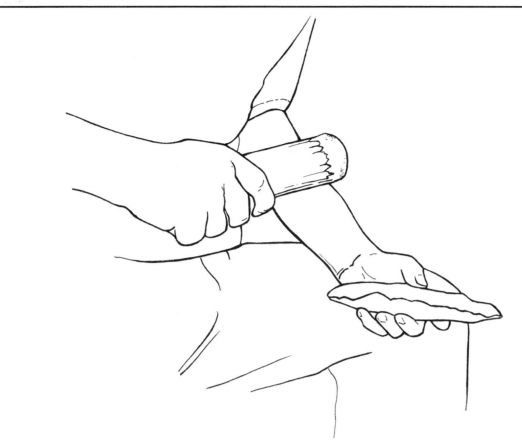

FIG. 41. *Another view of freehand percussion, this time using the antler billet.*

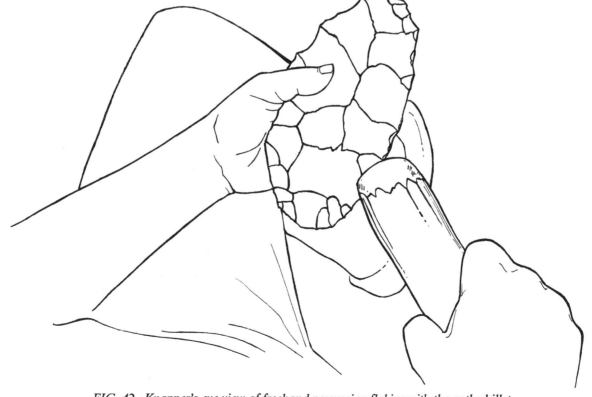

FIG. 42. *Knapper's eye view of freehand percussion flaking with the antler billet.*

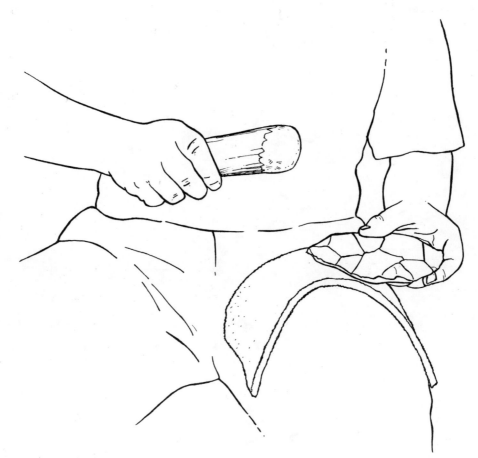

FIG. 43. *Percussion flaking with the moose antler billet while resting the preform on the leg. The holding position shown is for shorter flakes.*

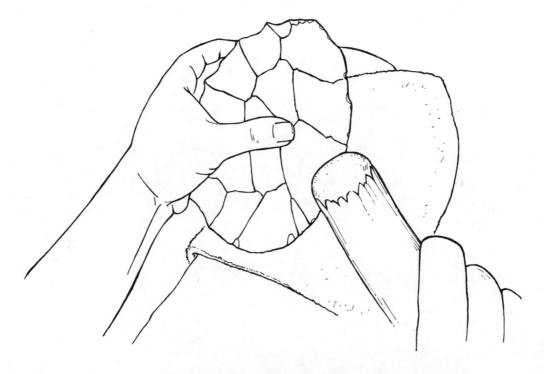

FIG. 44. *Knapper's eye view of percussion flaking on the leg pad.*

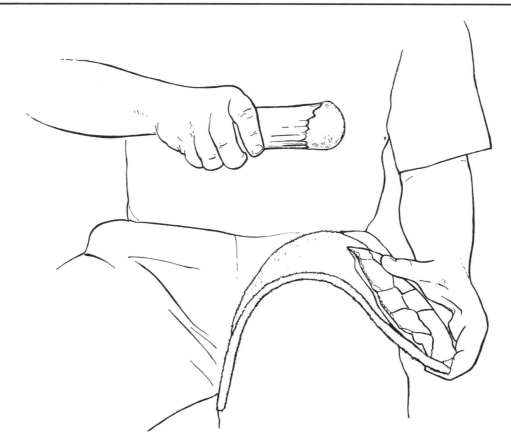

FIG. 45. *Another view of percussion flaking with the antler billet. This position will produce longer flakes. Note: The fingers are protected by the pad. This technique produces the same results as freehand percussion only with added safety.*

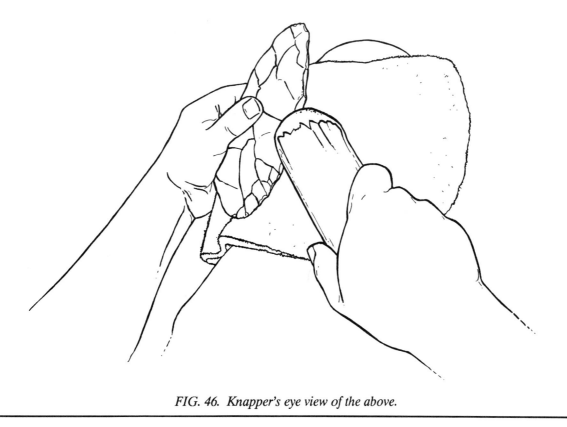

FIG. 46. *Knapper's eye view of the above.*

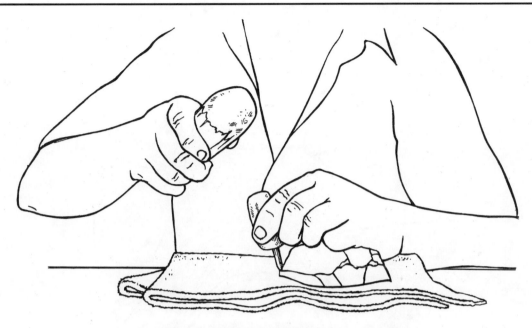

FIG. 47. *While punch flaking for heavy platforms the preform is supported on a soft pad on the bench.*

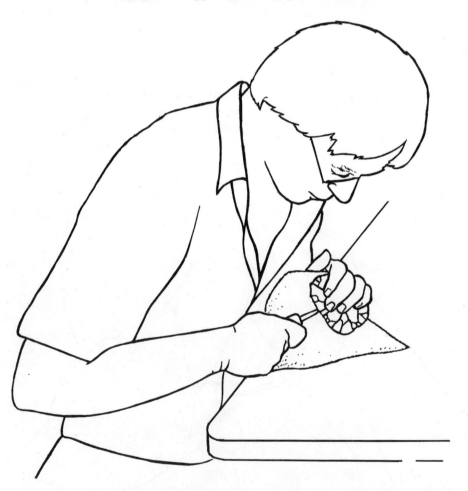

FIG. 48. *One of several bench rest holding positions used by the author. Here isolated platforms are being prepared on a medium sized preform. This same holding position can also be used for the removal of longer retouch flakes. Note: The pad is between the palm of the hand and the work.*

Chapter 6
FINISHING

Depending on the style of point that you wish to replicate the amount of pressure flaking as opposed to percussion will vary as the final series is removed. The surface of some Late Paleo and Early Archaic points may be almost completely covered with pressure flakes while those of Woodland points exhibit mostly percussion scars. However, due to their size, late period small arrow points are almost always pressure flaked. Since pressure flaking is a necessity for small point production as well as platform preparations, edge straightening and notching in the Late Archaic and Middle Woodland periods, this chapter will serve as an introduction to this technique. We will go into greater detail in the last chapters of this book.

The angles for pressure flaking are slightly different than those for percussion. With percussion, the edge is struck at 130 degrees to the expected flake while the direction for pressure is near parallel to the desired flake. I believe this greater angle is due to the fact that you actually have two forces at work. First you seat the tool and push inward, building up considerable pressure. Then while still pushing inward you press downward and the flake pops off. As with percussion the angles and placement of the tool tip will vary depending on the type and size of flake you wish to remove. After a little practice you should be pushing inward and downward with smooth strokes. Until you get the hang of it you might want to practice by making small arrow points from waste flakes.

As mentioned before, you must prepare the edge for pressure as was done for percussion. Because you are using a sharp tool and removing smaller flakes you will need a smaller platform. Here is a fast and sure way to prepare the edge: just scrape against it with the side of your pressure flaker by pushing downward and laterally. This action dislodges many small flakes in one stroke which is a lot faster than pushing them off one at a time. For special or heavier platforms used in parallel and oblique flaking it may be necessary to remove the flakes one at a time. Because most pressure platforms are less than 1/8 inch wide, you should grind but not too much. The pressure tool, be it copper or antler, will get a better bite if the bevel is left a little sharper.

Those of you who use carborundum abraders can grind in most of your platforms without any pressure flaking at all. However, you should avoid overdoing it. Also, one should avoid abrading in areas where final flakes have been removed. When cleaning up the edge in between large percussion scars you should grind and pressure flake only the junctures, thus maintaining a sharp edge on the final product. (If you intend to use your points for jewelry then the edges may be lightly abraded to dull them for safety's sake.)

The two basic holding-support techniques for pressure flaking are **free hand** and **bench rest**. In the free hand method the work is placed on a small leather pad in the palm of one hand while the other works the tool. Freehand chipping can be done standing or sitting, although the sitting position is most favored. More force can be generated by working between the legs and using an Ishi stick will further increase the leverage. I use the bench rest method the most. When you sit on a stool with your feet on the ground the bench top should be even with the pit of your stomach. If the work is placed any higher than this, you will not be able to get maximum leverage and after a short while you will probably strain your arm or your back. Because the work is rested on a stationary surface (using the leg pad as a cushion) you will be able to use most of your weight as well as all the power of your arm and shoulder.

Depending on the style, I believe that both of these methods and some variations were practiced in ancient times. I use a variation of both techniques when a bench is not available. I simply lay the piece on the pad on my knee and pressure flake it there. You may wish to experiment a bit to discover the technique that works best for you.

Once the basics of pressure flaking are mastered, notching of simple points like the Snyders-Hopewell is no big deal. It's the fancy E-notch, Lost Lakes, and dovetails from the Early and Mid-Archaic that can be real headaches if you don't know what you're doing. These will be dealt with in Chapter 9. For now I will show you how to make a standard narrow corner notch as well as the wider Woodland type.

To make a narrow notch place the point of your tool just above the edge at the place you want to notch and press to remove the first flake. Turn the piece over and remove the next flake from the platform formed by the first flake. From here you can remove more crescent-shaped flakes alternately until the notch has reached the proper depth. The strokes for notching are usually more downward than inward and the tool must be kept sharp. Wedge-shaped tools, both antler and copper, must also be properly maintained. These tools are pushed into the edge, thus seating them before the downward stroke is applied. In working a triangular preform with sharp corners the corners are first removed for better seating of the tool. Also, notching the thicker, more-difficult corner first enables the knap-

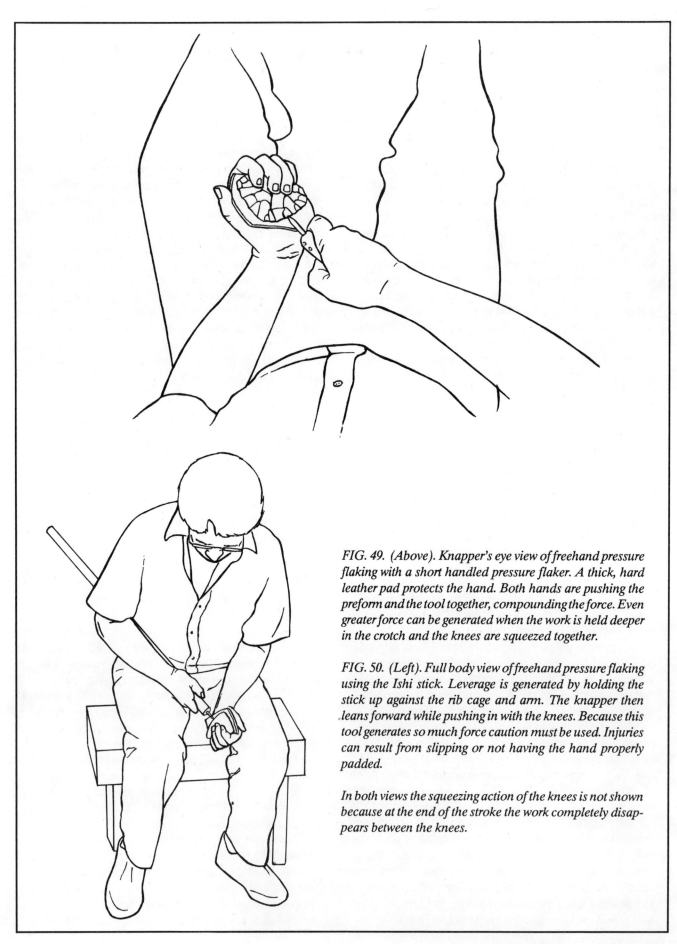

FIG. 49. (Above). Knapper's eye view of freehand pressure flaking with a short handled pressure flaker. A thick, hard leather pad protects the hand. Both hands are pushing the preform and the tool together, compounding the force. Even greater force can be generated when the work is held deeper in the crotch and the knees are squeezed together.

FIG. 50. (Left). Full body view of freehand pressure flaking using the Ishi stick. Leverage is generated by holding the stick up against the rib cage and arm. The knapper then leans forward while pushing in with the knees. Because this tool generates so much force caution must be used. Injuries can result from slipping or not having the hand properly padded.

In both views the squeezing action of the knees is not shown because at the end of the stroke the work completely disappears between the knees.

44

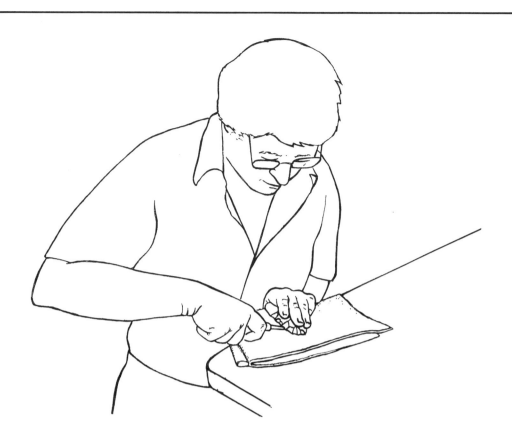

FIG. 51. *Pressure flaking on the bench. This is the safest of all pressure flaking methods. After several stokes the pad is cleared by picking it up and shaking the flakes off. If you brush them off with your hands you risk getting cut.*

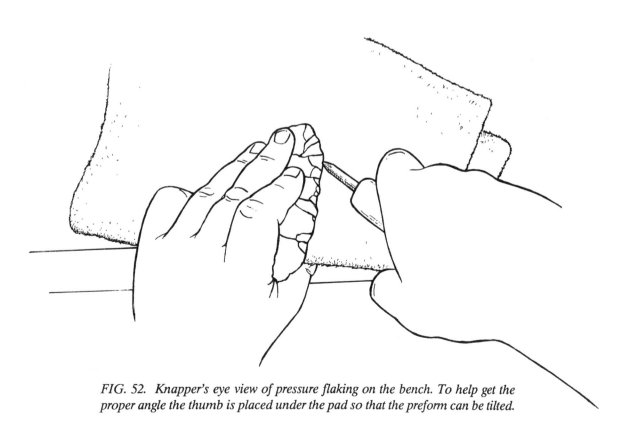

FIG. 52. *Knapper's eye view of pressure flaking on the bench. To help get the proper angle the thumb is placed under the pad so that the preform can be tilted.*

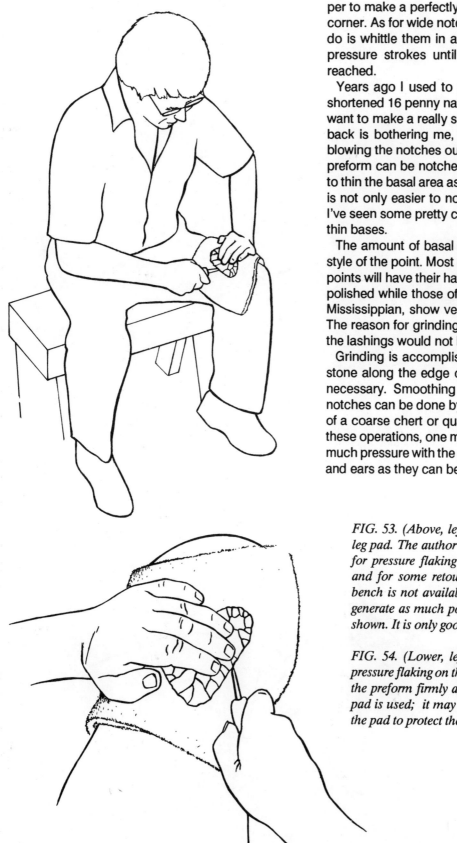

per to make a perfectly matching notch on the easier corner. As for wide notches and stems all you have to do is whittle them in and widen them out with short pressure strokes until the desired configuration is reached.

Years ago I used to punch my notches in using a shortened 16 penny nail and from time to time when I want to make a really super fine E-notch, or when my back is bothering me, I still do it. The advantage of blowing the notches out with a punch is that a thicker preform can be notched deeper, however, it is better to thin the basal area as much as you can. A thin base is not only easier to notch, but is also easier to haft. I've seen some pretty clunky old points that had nice, thin bases.

The amount of basal grinding is determined by the style of the point. Most of the Paleo and Early Archaic points will have their hafting areas heavily ground and polished while those of later cultures, Woodland and Mississippian, show very little or no basal treatment. The reason for grinding was to dull the edges so that the lashings would not be cut.

Grinding is accomplished by passing the abrading stone along the edge of the base as many times as necessary. Smoothing of the interior edges of the notches can be done by scraping them with the edge of a coarse chert or quartzite flake. While performing these operations, one must be careful not to apply too much pressure with the abrader, especially near barbs and ears as they can be fractured off easily.

FIG. 53. (Above, left). Pressure flaking on the leg pad. The author mostly uses this technique for pressure flaking platforms for percussion, and for some retouch and notching, when a bench is not available. This method does not generate as much power as some of the others shown. It is only good for shorter flakes.

FIG. 54. (Lower, left). Knapper's eye view of pressure flaking on the leg pad. The fingers hold the preform firmly against the leg. A thick soft pad is used; it may be necessary to double up the pad to protect the leg.

FIG. 55. NOTCHING

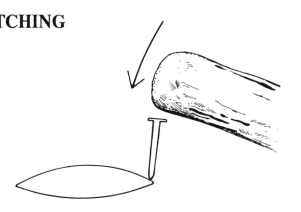

Notching with a punch. Placement is the same as with the pressure notcher except the angle is more perpendicular.

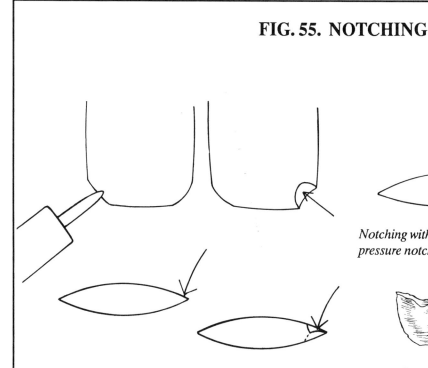

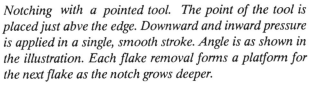

Notching with a pointed tool. The point of the tool is placed just abve the edge. Downward and inward pressure is applied in a single, smooth stroke. Angle is as shown in the illustration. Each flake removal forms a platform for the next flake as the notch grows deeper.

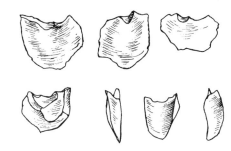

Notch flakes have a peculiar half-cone shape that makes them different from regular small pressure flakes.

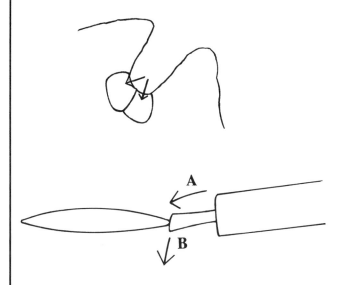

Wedge shaped tools, both antler and metal, are pushed into the edge, thus seating them, A. Then the downward stroke is applied to detach the flake, B. If the tool is kept sharp, slightly rounded, and free of deep nicks it will work better. Also, removing two flakes side by side helps to prevent hinging.

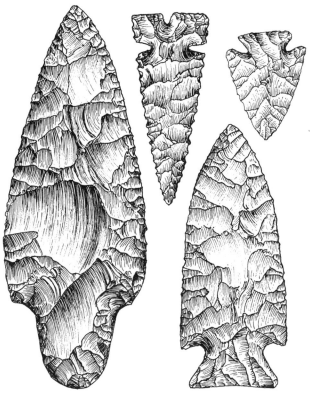

Simple stemmed and notched points from the midwest.

FIG. 56. *Raw materials commonly found in the midwestern United States.*
Sawed slab in the lower right hand corner is 10 inches in length.

FIG. 57. *Early stage preforms shown with medium and small hammerstones, and two large moose antler billets.*

FIG. 58. Late stage 4 and stage 5 preforms with small antler billets, pressure flaker, and abrading stone.

FIG. 59. Finished points and small 6 & 1/4" Type IV-A Danish dagger.

Chapter 7
TROUBLESHOOTING AND ADVANCED THEORY

In the last three chapters we have only hinted at potential problems. Thoroughly explaining the knapping process to this point has been difficult enough. However, the time comes for both the novice and the master to deal with these mis-haps. A single problem has the potential to ruin a project and when they come in combination it takes all hands and the cook to save the preform to get something out of it. Statistically, the larger and more complex a biface the more opportunities the lithic gremlins have. Whether it's a ten inch dagger or a one inch arrow point prevention is the best solution. However, until your skill has reached such a level that over 90% of your bifaces survive and come up to or very close to your expectations you will be referring to this chapter quite often.

Outside of hidden flaws in the raw material which can't be helped and excessive thickness which was dealt with in Chapter 5, we have: abruptly terminated fractures, edge crushing, overshot flakes, lipped flakes, and snap-breaks. In the following text each will be defined along with the cause, how to prevent the problem, and what to do about it when prevention has failed.

There are two types of **abruptly terminated fractures:** these are **hinge fractures** and **step fractures**. A hinge fracture occurs when the flake goes in and rolls out before feathering out, Fig. 60. With a step fracture the front continues on for a distance after the flake snaps out, Fig. 61. Both can be compounded if not removed before the next flake in the same area is attempted. Such compound fractures are referred to as **stacks,** Fig. 62. These problems are most often caused by angle miscalculations (striking too straight in) a blow that was not stout enough to carry the flake to completion, a pitted billet, or trying to drive a flake into a concavity on the surface of the biface. The best way to prevent the above is to learn to read your surface configurations, figure your angles and blows with greater precision and use billets sized and ground properly.

Edge crushing happens when trying to get a flake off an edge that is too thin or too sharp. In this case the hinges and steps occur very close to the margin. This is prevented by working back the edge to thicken it and by preparing platforms that will withstand the force.

When I first started knapping I had a lot of trouble with hinging and steps. To get at them I used to take a steel nail and set it against the step and try to punch off the remainder of the flake. I was sometimes able to remove smaller ones by pressure flaking with a copper pointed tool (antler pressure flakers don't work too well in this situation) after which the mess was cleaned up with the removal of more flakes by regular percussion. Larger steps required the removal of several flakes, Fig. 63. This method is fine for the beginner. However, the better flint knappers, both modern and prehistoric, use other techniques.

When the flake that comes off remains intact it can be put back into the scar and struck again like a punch, leaving only a slight ridge where the two flakes butted against each other, Fig. 64. I know for certain that this method was used in ancient times because I have seen several old specimens that bore the tell-tale scars left behind by such an operation.

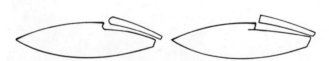

FIG. 60. Hinge fracture.   *FIG. 61. Step fracture.*

FIG. 62. Massive stack on an original artifact.

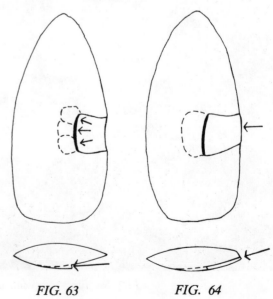

FIG. 63   *FIG. 64*

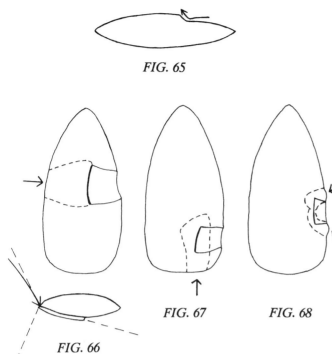

FIG. 65

FIG. 67   FIG. 68

FIG. 66

Lipped flakes happen when a half-moon shaped section of the edge comes out with the flake. Such flakes, when found, will have a distinctive "lip" attatched to the proximal end that was a part of the original preform margin, Fig. 72. Lips are the result of striking too high on the edge, or too stout a platform preparation on a thin edge. Also a higher percentage of lips occur when brittle, highly heat treated materials are used. To prevent lipped flakes, thicken the edge by working back the margin into thicker areas of the blade, and use smaller, isolated platforms that are relieved and below the center plane, and don't miss when you strike. If the preform has survived an overshot or lipped flake, the only thing you can do is reshape it.

There are certain step fractures that lean outward and you simply cannot get a hold of them with the punch or the pressure flaker, Fig. 65. In this case, if the biface is not too wide a flake can be removed from the opposite edge that will go across the face and catch the step from behind, Fig. 66. If the problem is near the base or tip it can be removed by a flake sent up the center of the blade, Fig. 67. For large, wide bifaces special isolated platforms will have to be prepared above and below the offending flake and two angled flakes driven off in an attempt to go around and under the hinge, Fig. 68. This is usually done for steps that are close to the edge. The only other choices are to grind them off or bore tiny holes in them with an electric engraver for the pressure flaker to catch hold of.

Overshot flakes usually occur when using isolated platforms, the curvature of the surface, and the support is just right for maximum flake travel; but the angle of the blow is too low. So, the flake goes all the way across the preform and takes out a section of the opposite margin, Fig. 69. The best way to prevent this is to back off on the angle and loosen up on the support. Overshot flakes can also occur during end thinning. These are called **roll out fractures** because the flake dives or rolls into the body of the preform. Fig. 70 shows the typical roll-out where the base and flake both have separated from the tip. Fig. 71 is more rare and usually occurs on thicker, narrower preforms, Here the base has rolled out but the flake stayed attatched to the tip. These types of failures are commonly associated with attempts at fluting Clovis and Folsom points. Again, back off on the angle or try thinning the base from the sides first.

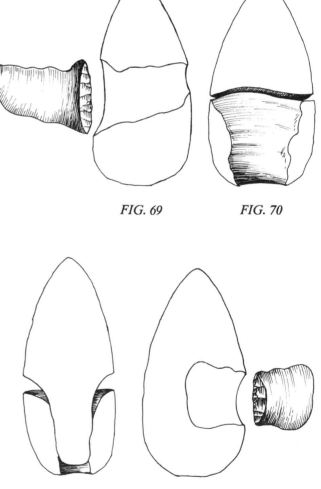

FIG. 69   FIG. 70

FIG. 71   FIG. 72

Snap breaks are clean fractures that halve the biface or cause a portion of it to suddenly detach. These are divided into two categories: end snaps, and shock breaks or lateral thinning fractures.

51

End snapping usually occurs on large bifaces over 4 inches in length. What happens is that you are working merrily along on one end and as you strike the other end falls off because the piece is not supported along its entire length. When working the ends of large preforms I support them along my outstretched leg. Fig. 73 shows this being done for a dagger blank. Note the heavy handle end is laying flat on top of the leg and the fingers are supporting the area where the flake is to come off. This dampens any excess shock that might be generated when the blow is struck. Fig. 74 is another view of this technique showing the leg pad in use.

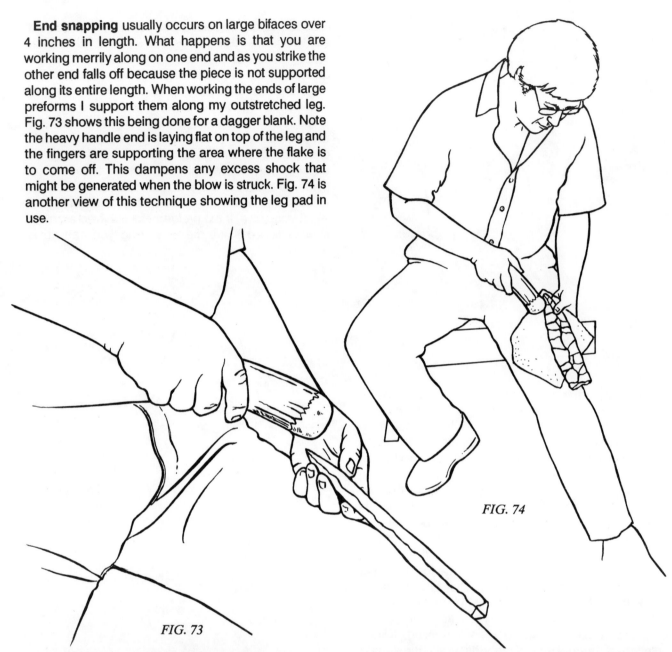

FIG. 74

FIG. 73

What I'm calling a **shock break** occurs during lateral thinning when the piece is snapped in two by a blow that exceeds the limits of the tensile strength of the stone. This happens sometimes without the flake coming off, but most often you are left with a nice flake and what will go on to become two small arrow points. Failures without flakes are caused by missing the platform and striking too high in the body of the biface or striking too hard. When the flake does come off and the piece still breaks then it was caused by a shock dampening and support problem.

Holding the blank edge-wise instead of flat will redirect the shock through the width of the blade rather than to its thickness. (Think about how a 2 x 6 beam will support more weight on edge than it will laying flat). The frequent use of well prepared, isolated platforms

below the center plane will lessen the chance of over-strike and the flake will detach and pull away before too much of the billet or excessive force is brought to bear.

If you are working on your leg the only problem with this position is the difficulty in striking accurately while leaning over to one side. To solve this the blow is **vectored**. In Fig. 75 the path of the billet has two components. A, coming almost straight into the platform and B, pulling back on impact. After the fracture is initiated the force changes and comes more in line with the correct angle. In the case of tough or grainy material it is possible to prolong contact before changing angles thus pumping more power into the piece. This is tricky and is best done with isolated platforms which are more forgiving than continuous ones. To

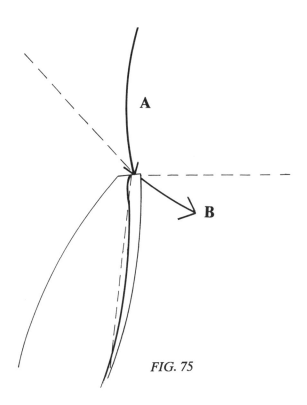

FIG. 75

perform the above consistently, without hinging, requires a good deal of practice for it all happens in less time than it takes to consciously blink an eye.

At this point, it becomes obvious that the use of certain holding positions and vectored blows is a way to bend the rules so that one can push the limits of size and width to thickness. In the following I will touch upon some advanced theory and practice, especially certain holding and support techniques such as "plant and strike", "open" or "closed support", and "trapping and pulling".

At first the preform should be held firmly, but not tightly. This can also cause breakage. By holding firmly excess movement is eliminated and shock is dampened. In addition to this I will sometimes use what I call the **plant and strike technique.** Here you plant the billet against the platform and push in hard and take a practice swing or two before striking in earnest. This helps to seat the blank firmly in the palm of the hand as well as impart a "memory" in your arm as to where the billet should fall. This really improves accuracy.

Another thing that could effect accuracy that was only touched upon in Chapter 5, Fig. 38, is how the billet is held when swung. It should be held loosely, but not so loose that it flies out of the hand. The elbow and wrist should not be stiff thus allowing for a fluid motion that will increase the speed of the swing. Smaller billets can be snapped against the edge with a quick, short

stroke which makes for a very accurate strike. This is why I depend upon them so much for medium to small bifaces as well as large thin ones when isolated platforms are used. Also, when contact is made the piece should be held solidly at the proper angle. Some beginners, those who work freehand in particular, have a tendency to let the preform drop a little as it is struck, thus changing the angle and throwing the flake off course.

Materials, preform size, length, and positioning of the flakes will determine what support or aid to flaking will be used. Holding the piece loosely or not supporting it where the flake is coming off is called **open support**. This is used when spalling cores, roughing thick, massive bifaces or running thick, short flakes for beveling platforms. **Closed support** is when the preform is held firmly between the thumb and fingers with the fingers supporting the area where the flake is coming off. The flake is **trapped** in place. By **pulling** on the flakes with the fingers their length may be extended from 25-30% depending on the material and the surface configuration. Where, when, and on what materials these techniques are used will come with experience. Modifications will be made by the individual according to comfort and style.

For my own comfort and safety I always work with a double sueded elk hide pad about 1/8 to 3/16" thick between me and the stone. Unlike the stiff leather pads used by others, this one is soft and flexible and allows enough feel that I can trap and pull with the best of the bare handers without the nicks and cuts and drying effects of flint dust that wreaks havoc with bare skin. As a result of this practice my hands don't look like they've been beating on stone for a quarter of a century.

Smaller bifaces, those under 5" long and 2" wide, will not require pulling unless the material is very tough. Closed support with a firm grip may be all that's needed. However, the grip should be less for brittle, well heat treated materials. Over controlling may cause diving and hinging, or at the least, unsightly hang nail flakes. On narrower bifaces overshooting is always a possibility.

Very large bifaces, on the other hand, will benefit from all the control tricks you have in your bag. Those in the dagger class, 10-14" or more, I work edge-up on the side of my padded knee, trapping and pulling while working in the center. For the ends I lay the piece along my outstretched leg, and carefully squeeze the area to dampen shock while the blows are dealt gingerly (see Fig. 45, 46, 73, and 74).

How do we know when the limits of the stone's ability to withstand the pounding is being reached without breaking it? First of all, if you strike with what you believe is an adequate blow and the flake does not come off, and you do this repeatedly without success,

FIG. 76. PLATFORM PREPARATION VARIABLES
(after Callahan 1979:34)

These two pages were part of the Third Edition. Though they are not level line drawings they are still handy for quick reference. All of these situations have been thoroughly discussed in the text. If you have a problem visualizing the angle, tilt the book or use an angle gauge as described in Fig. 77 & 78.

SHARPNESS OF EDGE

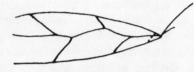

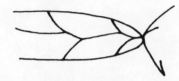

TOO SHARP
Edge may collapse or release small flake. Dull by abrading perpendicular and/or parallel to the lineal edge with coarse abrading stone.

CORRECT
Dull only enough to prevent collapse of platform. Correctly dulled, the flake should release with the first strike.

TOO DULL
Excessive resistance causes the billet to glance off without releasing the flake. Reflake to reduce thickness of the edge.

ANGLE OF BEVEL

TOO LOW
Edge may collapse. Rebevel to steeper angle.

CORRECT
Bevel to 60-70° so edge points slightly downward and flake releases on the first attempt.

TOO STEEP
Force may glance off. Rebevel to lower angle. Avoid continued striking.

PLACEMENT OF PLATFORM

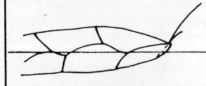

ABOVE CENTER
Flake may be short, or biface may break. A major cause of fracture. Lower the platform.

CENTERED
Flake may travel to center. Less chance of fracture. Ideal for primary thinning.

BELOW CENTER
Flake may span up to the entire width of the biface. Minimum chance of fracture. Ideal for secondary thinning.

ACCURACY OF AIM

TOO LOW
May either fail to release flake, crumble the platform, or yield flake smaller than desired. Aim higher.

CORRECT
Ideal contact point is about 1/8" back from the edge. Correct platform attributes help assure correct release despite slight inaccuracy of aim.

TOO HIGH
May either fail to release flake or break biface in two. A common cause of fracture. Aim lower.

STRIKING ANGLE

 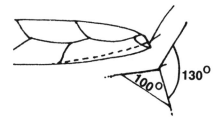 

TOO STEEP
May release short flake or glance off platform. Lower striking angle. This is ideal for trim between major flake removals.

CORRECT
Strike at 130° to the expected flake scar for optimum results.

TOO STRAIGHT IN
May split the biface with overshot or deeply hinged flake, or may produce partial cone and a crushed edge. A major cause of rejection. Raise striking angle.

CURVATURE OF SURFACE

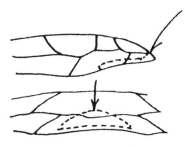 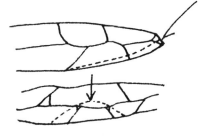 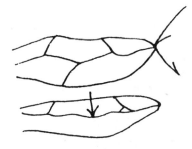

CONCAVE TO FLAT
Force may dissipate and flake may step or hinge upon encountering greater mass. Round off the overhang.

SLIGHTLY CONVEX
Allows for optimum removal of mass with least resistance.

OVERLY CONVEX
Excessive resistance preventing flake removal. Lower the platform or remove hump from another direction.

then rework the platform. It's too rounded or stout. The flake should release on the first or second impact with only a slight increase in amplitude. One can feel the stone vibrate when it is struck and large bifaces will ring like bells. If they ring loudly, the shock is not being dampened properly and it's only a matter of time before they are tolled into oblivion.

Other more subtle signs of stress which can actually be seen are **splits**. As discussed in Chapter 4, I believe that these are caused by slight bending of the preform when it is struck and the surface of the stone is stretched so that it splits. If the preform is bent too much one of these cracks will open up and the preform will fail. On tough Pedernales flint bifaces I have had these splits go a quarter of the way through without breakage. This was due to good support. These cracks were either chipped away as the blank was thinned past them, or they remained and the point was finished anyway. Again, due to proper support techniques, the piece survived. So if splits become obvious, especially in the tougher material, it's time to back off.

The size of the starting blank and the amount of flaking relevant to finishing it into the largest possible point is what I call the **reduction ratio**. Now I don't have figures and charts to back me up, but the principle is rather obvious. If the point can be finished to standard spec with 1000 flake removals as opposed to 2000 it will be much larger due to less platform preparations and fewer flakes struck off. A low reduction ratio represents greater efficiency and more conservative use of raw materials. If super thinness is desired then extra flakes will have to be taken off, beyond the normal number, thus upsetting this balance. Unless you start with an extra large blank or a very thin one the size will almost always be less than desired. The only way to beat this is to have all of your flakes come off near perfect, with every one doing its job of thinning and shaping.

Knowing the limits of the raw material you are using is critical to success. The Old Timers were well aware of width to thickness ratios vs. size and strength factors, and they knew when to quit while they were ahead. As your knapping skills improve your products should naturally get thinner with less hinging and more regular scar patterns. And as your efficiency in obtaining the above increases, so will the size until the barrier of diminishing returns is reached. From here it's a matter of luck. There is nothing wrong with consistently making a good quality replica that falls within the accepted perameters of the chosen type. In the beginning this is the goal we all seek. However, as we push the envelope of fineness and thinness to its limits it is our skill, at ever increasing levels, that more and more replaces luck.

FIG. 77. For those of you who are having trouble visualizing the correct angle you may wish to construct a Hertzian Cone angle gauge like the ones we used to help us with the level line drawings in this book.

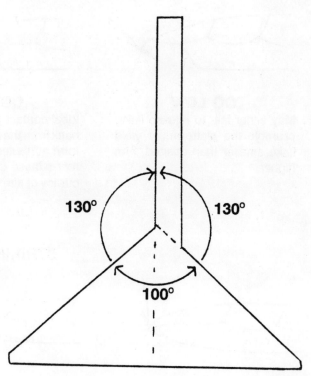

Cut 1/8" plexiglass to this shape (heavy lines). Scribe in dotted lines showing completed cone and angle of force with a needle or exacto knife point. Thin materials other than plexiglass may also be used.

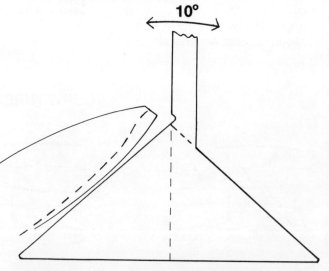

FIG. 78. To calculate angle of preform and angle of blow for standard holding position on the leg or in the hand, hold the gauge with the bottom level and lay the face of the piece against the cone as shown. The path of intended fracture should be roughly parallel to the side of the gauge. Note: Due to variations in percussors, platforms, and materials, a 10° margin of error should be allowed.

Chapter 8
FLAKE AND BLADE CORES

In the Old World core technology has a long history. It is marked by trends towards greater efficency, getting more and more edge per pound of flint. With better and lighter tools man was able to extend his range and make his life more comfortable. Here in America core technology was not so heavily relied upon. The biface manufacturing process produced plenty of flakes and blade-like spalls that could be saved and used, as is, or slightly modified to suit the purpose. Such artifacts are referred to as **utilized** or **modified flakes**, and they can show up in significant numbers when debitage from a site is properly analyzed. As far as true blade cores are concerned, here in the midwest there were two cultures that used them to such an extent that it shows up in their assemblages. The Clovis people worked large, conical and block cores as well as biface cores, and the Hopewell Mound Builders used smaller, more refined ones usually made from heat treated Flint Ridge or Burlington chert. Some Hornstone specimens are also known. As far as the survivalist and the black powder shooter is concerned this chapter is important because simple cores will yield blades for tools and gunflints with a minimum of skill required. First we will begin with a quick review of the technology as it developed in Europe.

Clactonian. The Clactonian is one of the best examples of the so-called chopper and flake industries that are found in various parts of the old world. The collections from which this industry gets its name came from Clacton-On-Sea in Essex, England. These tools are perhaps 200,000 to 300,000 years old which places them in the hands of Homo-Erectus.

The collection is divided up equally between the choppers which are the same thing as pebble tools and early hand axes and flake tools made from thick flakes having a pronounced bulb of percussion and ripples. Some of these flakes were the useful by-product of chopper manufacture while others came from crude cores which were worked in the following manner. First a flake was removed by striking the edge of a flatish nodule with a hammerstone. Then a series of flakes were removed alternately using the first as well as successive scars as platforms. This produced a core that resembled a large chopper, similar to the biface core shown in Chapter 5, Fig. 21. This has caused some controversy as to whether or not the Clactonian cores really are cores. However, there is no doubt that the flakes were modified by coarse retouch to form tools like side scrapers, notched shaft scrapers, denticulates (saws), some backed knives, and becs or boring tools. It is interesting to note that along with this collection of woodworking tools was found the pointed forward section of a wooden spear that had been fire hardened.

Levallois. Around 200,000 years ago the Acheulian hand axe makers began to develop and practice what has come to be called the Levallois technique. This involved the careful flaking of a flint nodule around its sides and top in preparation for the detachment of a massive flake of predetermined shape. In the examples illustrated, Fig. 79, the preliminary flaking of the top regulates the shape: circular or oval, rectangular, and pointed. These flakes were used with very little retouch. A flake as it comes off is as sharp as it will ever be. Retouching will only dull it. The Levallois technique will produce only about a dozen or so tools per core, if you are a fairly good knapper. In my opinion this technique is a bit complicated and wasteful. In fact, it seems to have been used more in regions where large flint nodules were abundant.

Mousterian. The Mousterian disk core is closely related to the Levallois and probably developed from it. Both were in use simultaneously during the Middle Paleolithic period (about 85,000 to 35,000 years ago) and were the hallmark of Neanderthal Man.

In the Mousterian technique the top of the core became the striking platform and the flakes were driven off the sides rather than off the top. This was continued around and around the nucleus as it became disk shaped, then finally too small to produce sizable spalls, Fig. 80. At this point the core was either discarded or an attempt was made to salvage it by making a small biface or scraper. Using a hybrid based on these two techniques, which no doubt they did also, I got 85 serviceable flakes from a nodule the size of a coconut. First I worked the top Levallois style for the large ones (4 inches long) and the sides Mousterian style for the smaller ones (3 inches or less). Also, this technique is well suited for working blocks because you simply use one of the flats as a platform (see illustrations in Chapter 5).

Before we go any further, I want to once again explain the difference between flakes and blades. A blade is at least twice as long as it is wide. A flake is broader and thicker. True blades have fairly parallel sides and are thinner with either a triangular or trapezoidal cross-section, depending on whether one or two scar juncture ridges are present on the dorsal face. Good blades coming from well prepared nuclei look somewhat like

FIG. 79. LEVALLOIS CORE

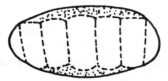 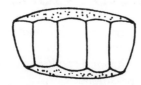 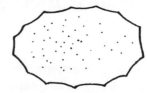 

The first step in making a Levallois core was the peripheral flaking of a flint cobble.

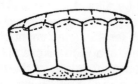 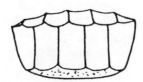 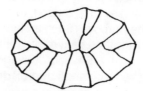 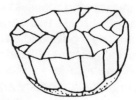

Next the top of the cobble was worked using platforms formed by the flakes removed from the sides.

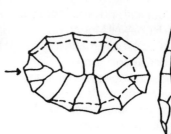

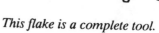

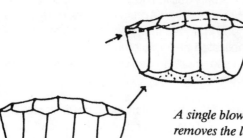

A single blow dealt at one end removes the large flake from the top.

This flake is a complete tool.

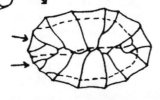 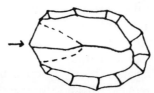 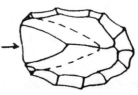

In making the Levallois point the two flakes are first struck to form a scar juncture ridge, after which a third thinning flake is struck. A fourth and final blow detaches the point.

These cores can be reworked by reflaking the top from the sides and repeating the above process.

FIG. 80. MOUSTERIAN CORE

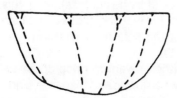

 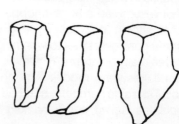

Mousterian cores were simpler than Levallois cores and yielded more flakes and blades. A half nodule was worked from the top with the blades coming off the sides. Removal was continued until the core was disk shaped.

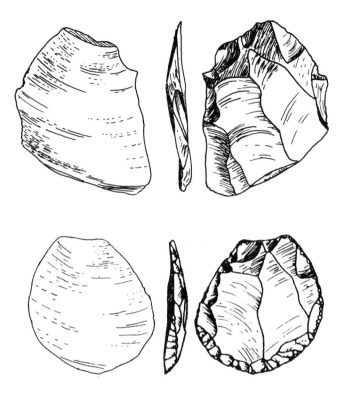

FIG. 81. Three views of a waste flake and a thumb scraper that was made from it.

of flakes and blades you will be able to replicate all of the points, tools, and gun flints shown in this chapter.

To make a core from a nodule you must first halve it if it is round, or knock the end off if it is egg-shaped, as mentioned earlier. A Mousterian disk-shaped core can be made from the flatter ones. Since blocks already have flat surfaces for striking platforms it's only a matter of deciding which one to use to get the best flakes or blades.

FIG. 82. UPPER PALEOLITHIC BLADE CORE

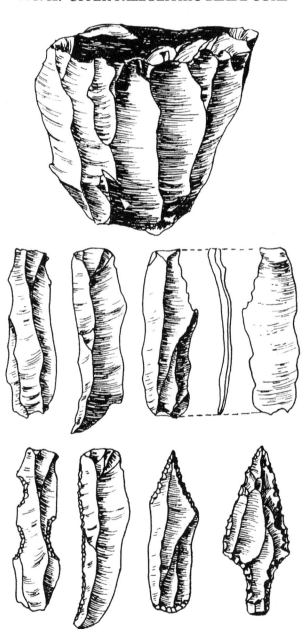

Conical prismatic blade core with blades and tools made from the blades (reduced 1/3). From left to right: a shaft scraper or denticulate blade, a backed knife, combination borer-end scraper, and a Font Robert point.

prisms. Thus, they are referred to as **prismatic blades**. They can be as large as 8 or more inches by 2 inches or as small as 1 by 1/8 inch. Those smaller than 2 inches by 1/2 inch are known as **bladelets**, and those coming off of tiny 1 inch cores are **micro-blades**.

Blades do occur in the Middle Paleolithic, sometimes as a result of the Levallois and Mousterian techniques. Under the right conditions these two methods will produce a certain number of blades. However, the majority of such artifacts come from the Upper Paleolithic and later periods.

Prismatic Blade Cores. Early cores were worked by direct percussion with hammerstones. An antler billet could also have been used. This tool might have led to the production of thinner and longer flakes that could be classed as blades. A further refinement would have been the use of indirect percussion with an antler punch being struck by the billet, or pressure flaking on smaller cores. The last two methods allowed for much greater control of force application leading to the development of conical, prismatic blade cores that could produce long, thin, parallel sided blades, Fig. 82.

Making your own prismatic blades is fairly simple if you patiently follow these directions and practice a bit. Don't worry if you are not able to make all of the blades perfect. The old timers didn't either. With a good supply

A block or nodule can be trimmed to shape by direct percussion with an antler or hammerstone. Large flakes produced by trimming will be useable with the first ones off a nodule having a cortex adhering to the outside. Some may be nearly all cortex and will have to be discarded. At this stage it is possible to continue working the core with the stone or the antler as I often do. If you become adept at percussion you can make some very good blades this way.

After every series of blade removals it will be necessary to trim off the overhang and the sharp points at the junctures around the periphery of the top of the core. If not removed the overhang will get in the way of the next series. This can be done by light percussion or pressure followed by abrading. Sometimes the top of the core in the area where it is to be struck is also abraded. Roughing up the slick surface a bit causes the tool to get a better bite without slipping. Also, this scratching will weaken flint and especially obsidian, just as a glass cutter's scratch will weaken glass, making it easier to break. Tests have shown that about 10% less force is required to cause a fracture where the platform is abraded (Patterson 1981:8). This is a good enough reason to abrade all platforms whether it be on a core or on the edge of a biface.

Placement of the blow or the punch on the platform and the angle at which the blow is delivered or the tool is held is crucial. For wider, thicker flakes and blades the blows are struck farther from the edge. Thinner, narrower ones result when striking closer to the edge. Blades that are triangular in cross-section are made by striking so as to have only one scar juncture present on the dorsal face. A trapezoidal blade includes two.

The tool is placed on the platform in line with the blade to be, and then leaned inward a bit before the strike, Fig. 83. Percussion blows are dealt at nearly the same angle as the tool is held. When removing blades by pressure the pressure is first applied downward with a lesser outward force, initiating the fracture. Some practice and experimenting will be required to learn the correct angle and amount of force necessary.

There are several ways to hold a core while it's being worked. For direct percussion it's easily held in the hand or rested on the leg as you would do for a large biface. Tiny micro-blade cores can be hand held or rested on a bench while using the pressure flaker. When punching, I hold the core between my knees and cradle it in the leather pad. This protects my legs while helping to prevent slipping, Fig. 84. If necessary, further stabilization can be achieved by placing a long piece of heavy cloth under the core and over the knees. The cloth should be long enough to go down the outsides of your legs and under your feet. The downward force on the core will pull the cloth tight, thus pulling the knees closer together.

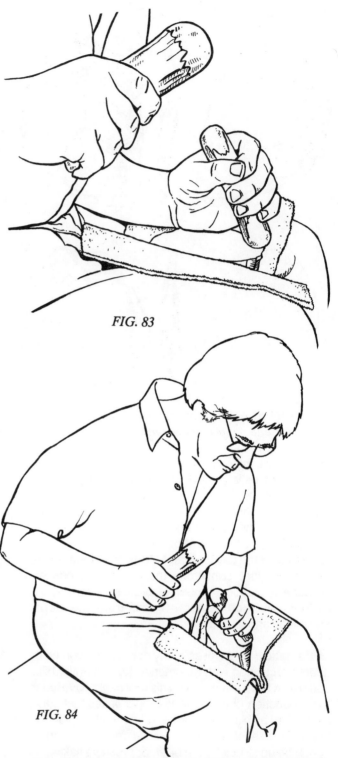

FIG. 83

FIG. 84

If I were lost in the wilderness I would use direct percussion on a Mousterian type core. With a hammerstone I could easily obtain all the blades and flakes of various shapes and sizes that I would need. Most of the tools shown in the illustrations were made from flakes and blades that came from both Mousterian and later Perigordian cores. All except the burin, Fig. 85, are easily made by simply reworking the edges by light percussion or pressure.

FIG. 85.   MAKING A BURIN

The burin, with its strong, chisel-like point, was the flint equivalent of a modern steel engraver. It was used to score deep parallel or V-shaped grooves in a length of antler or bone to isolate slivers that were pried out and worked into needles and spear points.

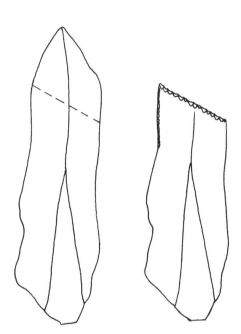

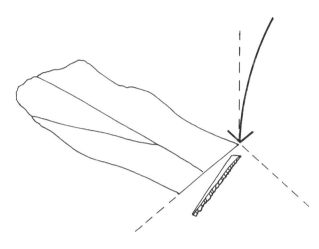

B. *Then a prism-shaped flake is removed from the point by pressure or percussion.*

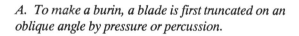

A. *To make a burin, a blade is first truncated on an oblique angle by pressure or percussion.*

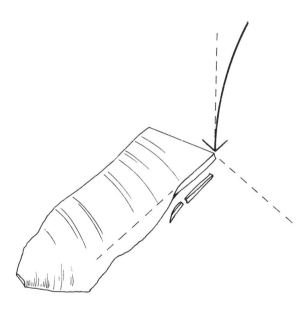

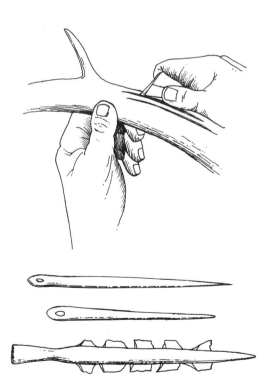

C. *To form the chisel point a second flake is struck down the side of the blade.*

D. *Using the burin to cut out slivers of bone or antler for the manufacture of needles and Magdelanian point.*

61

Before leaving this chapter I want to put in a word about gun flints for my friends who are fans of the flintlock. Being a blackpowder fiend myself, I have attended my share of shoots and rendezvous where I've made and traded a lot of flints.

FIG. 86. MAKING GUN FLINTS

A flintlock.

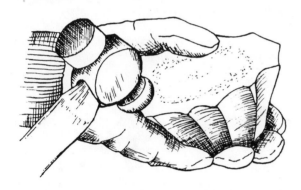

Striking the core with the ball-peen hammer.

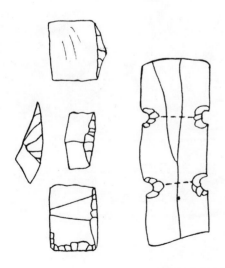

Making gun flints from a blade.

You can make your own flints by working your cores in the same way you did for blades and flakes. If you wish, you may try a steel hammer. A small, modified geologist's pick, mason's hammer, or ball-peen hammer (striking with the ball end) will work. A soft steel hammer like the one shown in Fig. 86 works even better. The one illustrated is patterned after an old English knapper's hammer that was made of iron. This hammer works very well when it comes to accurately pecking off the type of blades used for gun flints. The soft steel has more give than the harder metal of other hammers, which tend to shatter the stone.

After your blades are struck off you can truncate them by pressure chipping opposing notches into the edges of the blade. Then lay them on a pad and give them a rap. They should crack from notch to notch. Now trim the edges where the break occurred and you have a gun flint.

In order to get more shots out of a flint, you can remove it from the jaws and resharpen it by chipping a new edge. You can do this until the flint becomes too short to strike the frizzen properly.

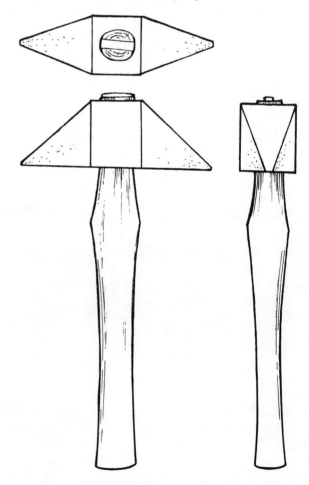

An English gun flint knapper's hammer made from mild steel.

Chapter 9
SOME NORTH AMERICAN BIFACES

This last chapter is for the knapper who has conquered the stage 5 biface and has learned the basics well. Here I will show you how to reproduce some of the better known artifacts while at the same time giving you some more tips and information. Most of these points and tools are from the the midwestern USA. Since they are in chronological order you will find the most complicated ones coming first which is a phenomena peculiar to the American archaeological record. Here it will be assumed that the reader is already somewhat familiar with these types and the roll they played in prehistory.

Clovis points. There are several types of fluted points and several different ways to flute them. **Fluting** is the process in which a large flake is driven off both faces from isolated platforms centered on the base. On Clovis points these **channels** usually extend 1/3 to 1/2 the length of the point and they accomplish both basal thinning and provide a groove into which the shaft settles. Since notches had yet to be developed, the lashing was simply wrapped around the base, glue was applied and the whole thing became quite solid.

The fluting technique I am about to discuss is perhaps the oldest and the simplest. It requires no fancy lever devices and other slick tricks which would take another book the size of this one to describe adequately. It works for points 2" long on up to a 9" Wenatchee style Clovis, and can be easily mastered by the intermediate knapper.

The "average" Clovis stage 5 preform should be about 3" to 3 & 1/2" inches long and 1 & 1/4" wide, with a W/T ratio of about 5/1. The longitudinal cross-section should taper slightly from the midpoint toward a base that is about 2/3 the thickness of the center while the distal end tapers to a blunted tip. It should be well flaked by percussion, then smoothed by random pressure. The pressure work will cover almost all the surface, thus producing the desired smoothness. Preforms can be thicker or thinner, but not having a W/T ratio greater than 4/1 or lesser than 6/1. After fluting and retouch the average finished Clovis point will be about 1/4 to 1/2 inch shorter and about 1/8 to 1/4 inch narrower than the original preform. No matter what the size the length to width ratios are about 3/1.

The first fluting platform is prepared by carefully chipping a rounded stem or **nipple** on the base, after which it is ground moderately to heavily, Fig. 87-A. For best results in fluting the edge at the tip of the nipple should lie below the center plane, but not quite even with the highest point on the median hump, Fig. 87-B.

If it is too high or too low, depending on the angle and weight of the blow, the flute will be too narrow or too short, or hinge deeply before traveling the desired distance. A too sharp or pointed nipple will be crushed, or if it is cracked or flawed it will also fail. The material that the blank is made of will determine the strength of the nipple; it should be heavier for weaker or grainier stone. What are called guide flakes can be chipped off the base at each side of the nipple further isolating it. This is usually done to a greater degree for the second flute. At this stage the blank may resemble a basal notched point with shallow, wide notches.

The blow that detaches the flute is carefully but firmly dealt to the nipple. If it is too straight in the platform will be crushed or a rollout fracture will shear the piece in two. If the angle is too steep the flake will feather out and not travel far enough. The ideal flute will be broad, run 1/3 to 1/2 the distance to the tip, and will terminate in a slight hinge, Fig. 87-C. The size of the billet and how the preform is held or supported also makes a difference.

For fluting all sizes of Clovis points, I have found a medium moose billet to be the most effective. A larger, slower moving percussor will prolong contact so the channels will actually run farther. However, don't use such a big billet that it overpowers the job or clips one of the ears when the second channel is being removed.

I have two support techniques that I now use almost exclusively because they work so well for me. Points under 3 & 1/2 inches are held firmly with the thumb under the pad and all the fingers on top, Fig. 88 & 89. For larger preforms 4 to 6 inches I use what I call the "spider hold", with the little finger pressed against the tip to keep it from flying off, Fig. 90 & 91. Also I leave these larger preforms thick and unfinished from the center on out so the piece is stabilized by its greater mass. On huge Wenatchee points I leave the distal 2/3 of the preform in late stage 3 while the basal end is thinned and tapered to stage 5 proportions. After fluting, the rest of the piece is thinned and shaped to the proper dimensions while care is taken not to invade the channel scars. This is the secret to making percussion fluted Clovis points 8 or 9 inches long with 6/1 or even 7/1 width to thickness ratios.

After the first flute is successfully removed a new nipple is prepared for the second, Fig. 87-D. Because of the deep hollow left by the bulb of the first flake, it is often necessary to work back into the base in order to form a thick enough platform. When this is done the ears will often protrude beyond the nipple. They should be trimmed back so that one of them will not be struck

FIG. 87. MAKING A CLOVIS FLUTED POINT

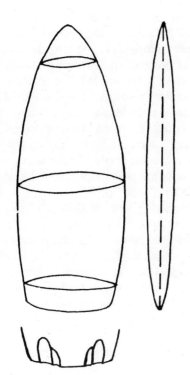

A. Preparing base.

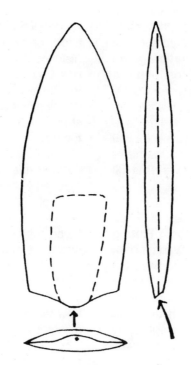

B. Removing first flute.

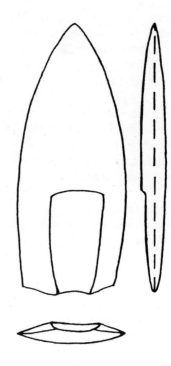

C. First flute removed.

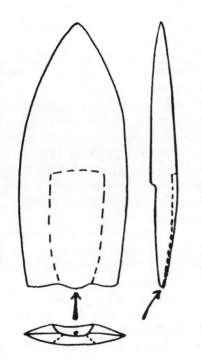

D. Removing second flute.

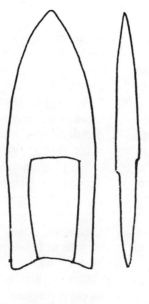

E. Finished point.

F. Long guides.

G. Striking the flute.

SUPPORT TECHNIQUES FOR FLUTING POINTS

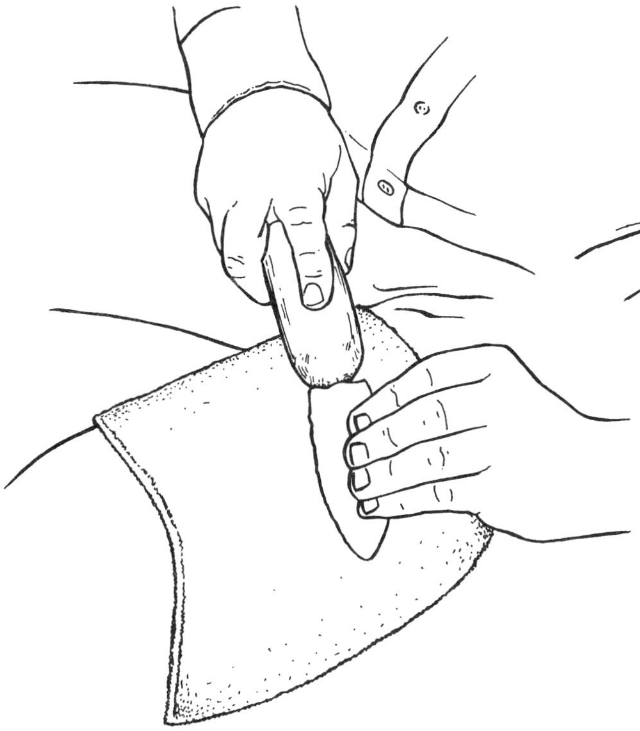

FIG. 88. Holding a small fluted point preform against the leg pad while striking the channel. Note: the fingers are on top of the preform.

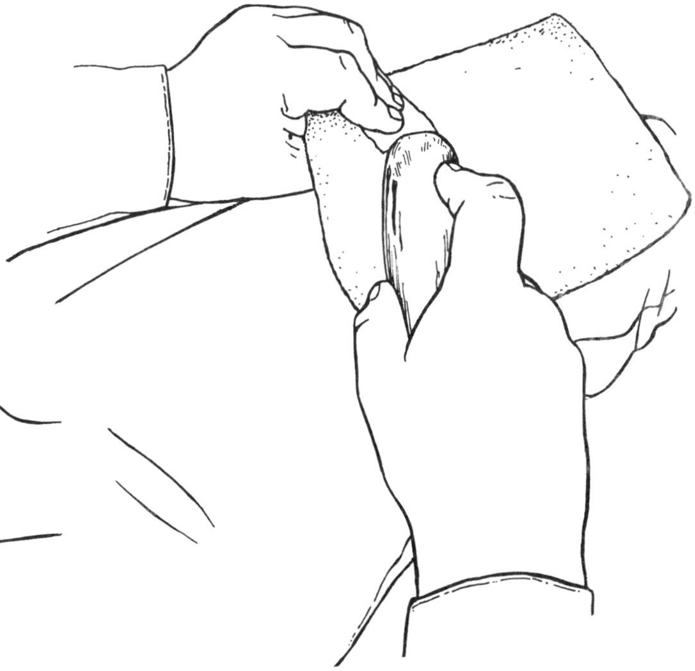

FIG. 89. Knapper's eye view shows the thumb under the pad and the fingers on top of the preform.

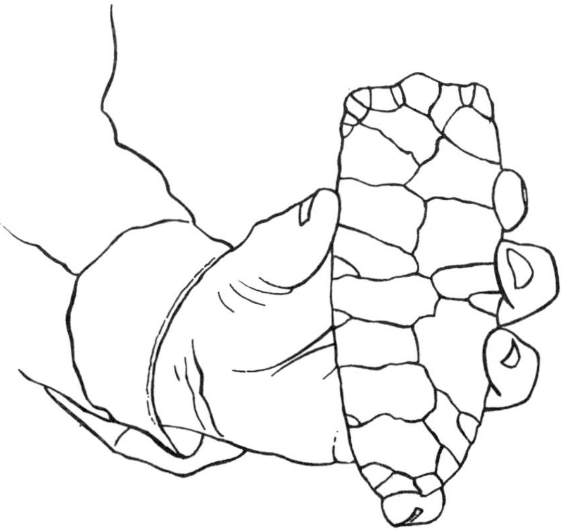

FIG. 90. "Spider" holding technique for large preforms. Note: the little finger pressing against the tip.

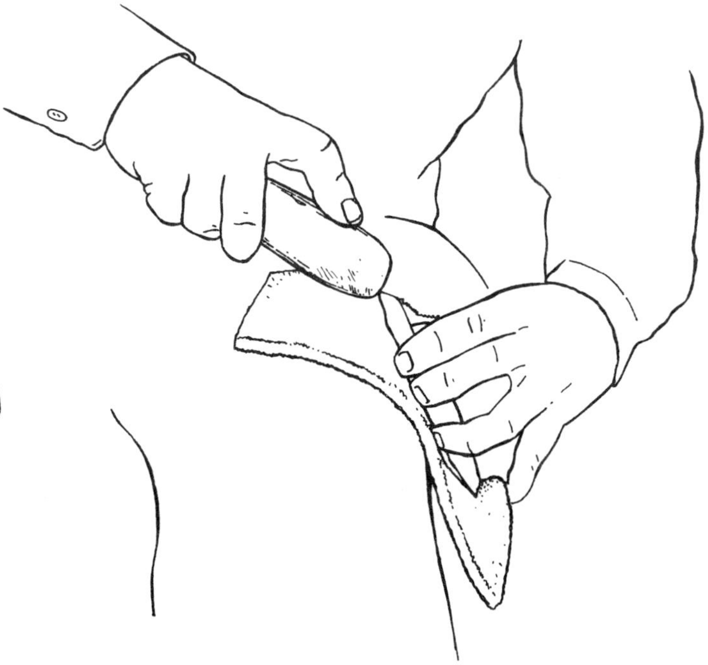

FIG. 91. "Spider" hold against the leg pad while using the pad to protect the little finger. If gloves are not used the edges of the preform should be abraded.

by accident. If all of this is done right the nipple should again lay below the center plane, but still not even with the median ridge.

After the second flute is removed both scars should taper back to a knife edge at the base. Then the point can be finished to the desired configurations after which the basal concavity and lateral edges in the hafting area are heavily ground, Fig. 87-E.

Now the biggest problem with fluting a point of any size is rollout fractures as discussed earlier. If they are not caused by mis-strikes or improper support, then certain surface configurations on the basal area are the culprits. The fact that fracture fronts travel well in areas of high relief is illustrated quite nicely when a channel flake follows a median ridge. If this ridge is well defined, in the case of the narrow preform with a width to thickness ratio of 4/1, the flake will go long. On the other hand, a wider preform of 5/1 or with an even flatter lenticular cross-section will cause the flake to spread. If it spreads too soon after initiation it will hinge short or roll out. This may be controlled by further isolating the nipple with **long guide flakes** driven off the base from near the corners, Fig. 87-F . On the second flute, if the ears are too long, I may rework them into tiny platforms for the guides, thus solving two problems at once. By the time the fracture gets out of this restricted area, usually 1/2 to 3/4 of an inch, its width and depth is pretty well set and it rides up nicely onto the blade without excess spreading, Fig. 87-G.

If you must attempt a Clovis start small and work up to larger points as you get the feel. Most beginners try fluted points long before they can make a good clean preform of the proper dimensions. If you can make the preform 100% your fluting survival rate should be 80%. However, don't expect the channel flakes on all of your points to be the same length on both sides. This is one of the hardest things to do. One can use a very thick preform and it will survive but the flutes are often too narrow, and they will not taper back to the base and form a sharp edge as that found on originals.

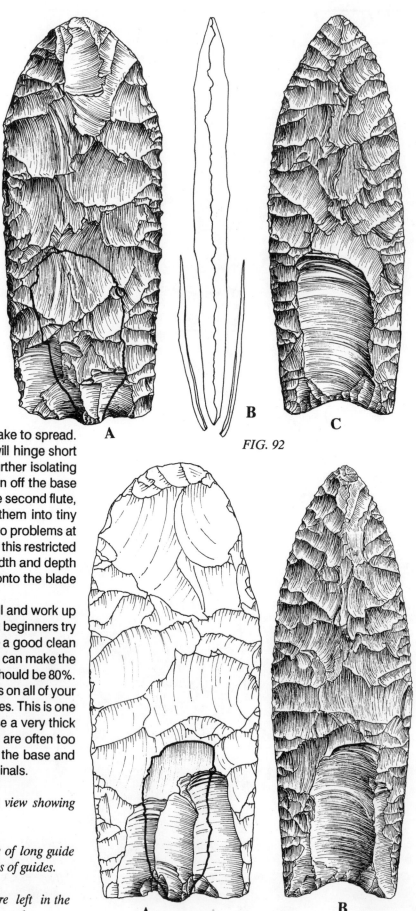

FIG. 92. *(A) Fluted preform. (B) Side view showing channel flakes. (C) Finished point.*

FIG 93. *(A) Fluted preform showing use of long guide flakes. (B) Finished point. Note remnants of guides.*

Both of these points due to their size, were left in the rough while fluting and the spider hold was used.

Lanceolate points. Lanceolates are long and narrow with a lenticular or diamond-shaped cross-section and have no flutes or notches. Some have broad stems, most all have basal grinding in the hafting area. The western varieties are pressure flaked over 80 to 100% of their surface. Eastern varieties are cruder in appearance because they are pressure flaked to a lesser degree.

There are two basic types of pressure scar patterns, **parallel** as found on Plainview, Agate Basin, Scottsbluff and Eden points, and **oblique** as seen on Brown's Valley, Allen, Angostura, and some large Daltons. Variations on these patterns are governed by cross-sectional configurations (median ridged, thin or thick lenticular) spacing of flakes, (wider or closer, more ribbon-like) and angle (horizontal or more or less oblique).

The average lanceolate is about 2 & 1/2 to 4 inches long. Those with heavy cross-sections will be narrower, 3/4 to 1 inch or so, and the lenticular ones will be wider. Seldom will you find a lanceolate wider than 1 & 1/2 inches because the length of pressure flakes removed by the average person is only 1/2 to 3/4 of an inch.

First you must start with a good, smooth stage 5 or late stage 4 preform slightly larger than the finished product. Off of this the initial series of pressure flakes will be taken. They will be removed more or less at random in order to erase the scar juncture ridges formed by earlier percussion. As you work over the blade it will get smoother and the flakes will become more uniform. It may take two or more sets from each face to accomplish this.

For a lenticular cross-section the biface is worked on a soft, padded surface or in the pad-protected hand. This padding is necessary when doing ribbon flaking because it supports and confines the flake helping it to curve in an arched trajectory over the median toward the opposite margin. For oblique flaking the tool is held at an oblique angle to the edge as opposed to right angles for comedial flaking.

To get a diamond-shaped cross-section the work has to be done in such a way that the pad or the fingers do not come in contact with the surface where the flakes are coming off. Because they are not held, they will not bend and go over the median, thus forming a sharper ridge. To do this I simply hold the piece in such a way that the median does not come in contact with the pad. For those of you who work in your hand, slotted blocks made of wood, as used by Bruce Bradley and Errett Callahan are good holding devises that work well for this type of flaking, Fig. 94 & 95. They can be placed in the palm of the hand with the preform held on top. The flake that is being removed falls through the slot and the piece is then repositioned for the next flake.

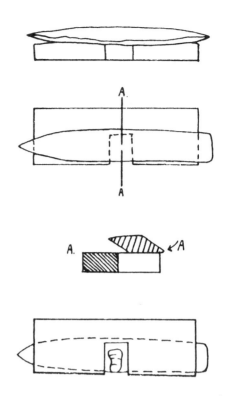

FIG. 94. Bradley's block.

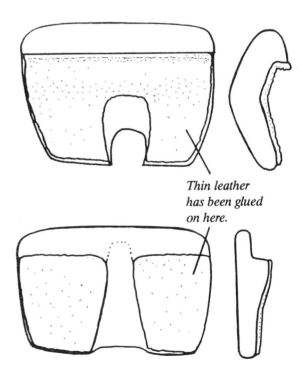

Thin leather has been glued on here.

FIG. 95. Callahan's blocks.

The last series of flakes should be removed slowly, paying close attention to spacing, platform preparation and direction of sequence. By controlling the spacing of the placement of the tool tip you will also be able to control the width of the flakes: closer for narrower flakes and farther apart for wider. For very narrow ones the tool must be kept relatively sharp.

Platform preparation is done by beveling the entire edge to the face opposite that to be flaked and then shearing by scraping the edge the other way with the shaft of your pressure flaker. This is followed by grinding the bevel, the shear, and the edge, making a good, hefty seat for the tool tip, Fig. 96. For the last series of flakes if the tool is placed high on the platform, when the flake is removed a small portion of the face will go with it. This leaves a razor-like edge, Fig. 97.

The rule for sequencing of oblique flakes as it applies to me when I work on the bench is this: start at the farthest pont on the margin, away from yourself (base or tip makes no difference), and work toward yourself. In other words, push the flakes AWAY on an oblique angle while working (progressing) into the mass to be removed by that series, Fig. 98. If you go opposite this it will take more force and the flakes will fan out or hinge, and a nice oblique pattern will not be formed easily, if at all. A good example of this principle can be found in shelling corn. If you hold the cob with its base nearest your belly and try to push the kernels off from that end they don't come off too easily. However, by pushing off the first one at the other end each consecutive kernel will fall into the space left by the last one. So each flake easily follows the ridge left by the last. If other holding positions are used then some experimentation may be necessary. For comedial parallel flaking the sequence is the same but, the angle is at 90 degrees to the median instead of oblique.

After the final series on the blade the base is finished by pushing off three or four flakes from the bottom margin to thin it and bring it to an edge. This is followed by a little more pressure work to form a stem, if that particular point has one, or by heavy grinding which often forms a slight stem.

Before leaving this section I want to make a few comments on oblique flaking. First of all, when you have mastered this technique you will find yourself using it for most of your pressure work because this method removes more stock in fewer series and in less time than random pressure flaking. If you are attempting to make authentic replicas, you should remember that this technique was only used on certain points and not on others. However, if you are a primitve bow hunter interested in results this technique will produce the sharpest edge of any style of bifacial flaking.

On a smooth preform you may need only one pass with a series of obliques to get a satisfactory finish. A second will further level the surface and even the

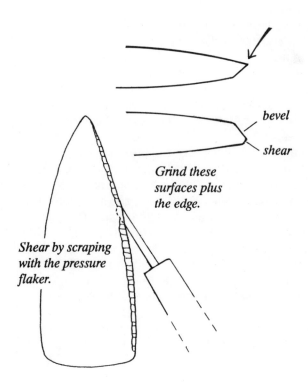

Grind these surfaces plus the edge.

Shear by scraping with the pressure flaker.

FIG. 96. *Platform preparation.*

FIG. 97. *Working high on the platform will remove a portion of the face leaving a razor edge.*

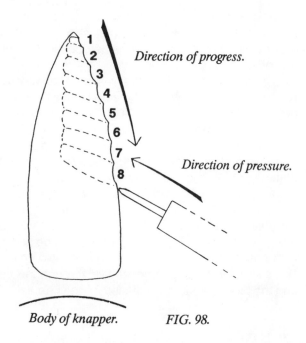

Direction of progress.

Direction of pressure.

Body of knapper. FIG. 98.

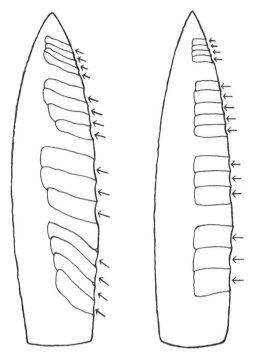

spacing a little more. A third series, if carefully controlled, will produce a near perfect pattern of tiny 1/16 inch wide, ribbon-like flakes. If the surface of the preform is ground smooth to the proper contour for optimum flaking the pattern will be so perfect it will look artificial. Such work may be seen on Type I-C Danish daggers and Egyptian Gerzian knives. Though this technique is unknown to the American archaeological record, many modern knappers have gone to using sawed and ground preforms because they can produce perfect points without the difficult and somewhat wasteful task of preforming by percussion. This is especially true for the use of expensive and hard to work gemstones.

FIG. 99. Angles and spacing for oblique and comedial parallel flaking.

FIG. 100. Angles of force application for lenticular and diamond shaped cross-sections.

FIG. 101   *FIG. 102*   *FIG. 103*   *FIG. 104*

Oblique and parallel flaked points: FIG. 101, Dalton; FIG. 102, Brown's Valley type;
FIG. 103, Agate Basin; FIG. 104, Scottsbluff Type I with heavy diamond cross-section.

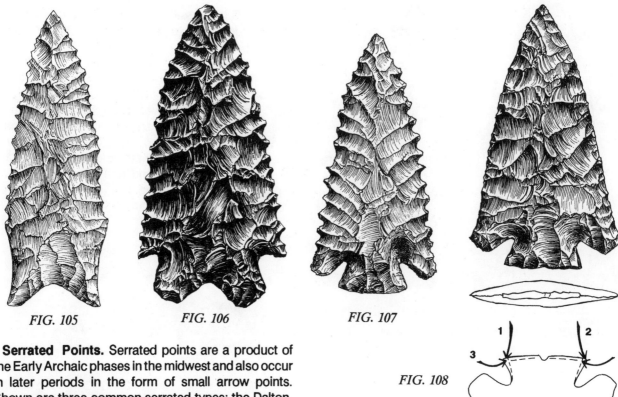

FIG. 105 FIG. 106 FIG. 107

FIG. 108

Serrated Points. Serrated points are a product of the Early Archaic phases in the midwest and also occur in later periods in the form of small arrow points. Shown are three common serrated types: the Dalton, Fig. 105, from both the Late Paleo and Early Archaic is often beveled as well as serrated; the MacCorkle lobed base point, Fig. 106; and Pine Tree corner notched, Fig. 107.

On these points the serrations are made by accentuating the flake scar junctures. This is accomplished by leaving the edge ragged after pressure flaking and by carefully hollowing out the spaces between the junctures where larger serrations are desired. Note: the edges in between the junctures in some areas may be a little too sharp for clean flake removals, and it may be necessary to grind them a bit. To get into the hollows without touching the serrations a thin piece of sandstone or a quartzite flake can be used.

Fractured Base Points. Fractured base points, also known as Decaturs, are found throughout the southeast and the Ohio Valley. For years people thought that this fracturing was due to mishap rather than intention because they resemble corner notched points with broken bases.

Basal fracturing is easily accomplished if these steps are followed with care, Fig. 108. First, chip a small notch or bifurcation into the center of the base. This serves as a stop so that when a burin-like flake is pushed off from the corner it will not continue and remove more than is intended. Next, two tiny flakes are taken off the sides of the stem from the corners by pressure. This aides in the removal of the two longer burin flakes which are also removed by pressure. I have found that without these squared platforms it is

difficult to get a flake to come off straight across. Usually it will bend to one side instead. Also, the proper angle must be used or the flakes will fall short or hinge out. The last step is grinding the base and the notches. Most specimens I have seen have such heavy grinding and polishing that it nearly erased the ripple patterns on the facets.

I believe that most Decatur points were used as knives or skinners since a great many specimens were resharpened by beveling. Because of the short stem and tiny notches one could not get much stability from lashing. Hafting was probably accomplished by cutting a square bottomed notch in the intended handle to match the square base after which the point was glued in place and some lashings applied. This would provide a stable haft that would prevent the tool from shifting while in use.

Beveled Points. Beveling or unifacial resharpening is also mostly an Archaic trait appearing on Dalton, Thebes, Lost Lakes, E-notches, corner notches, leaf-shaped, triangular knives, and some dovetails.

Bevels tell an interesting story if you know how to interpret them. To find out whether the maker of the point was right or left handed hold the specimen by the base with the tip pointing out. If the bevel of the right hand edge is facing down and you can see the one on the left edge, possibly the Indian was right handed. While resharpening the blade he held it with the tip pointed away from him. If he was a lefty the bevel would appear on the right hand margin. Now to further complicate the matter there is an exception to this rule. The Dalton was held pointing toward the Indian when he was resharpening it so just the opposite will apply to a right handed Dalton.

No matter if you're left or right handed, you can still get more resharpenings if you bevel your tool than if you resharpen it bifacially.

Beveling is accomplished by removing a series of flakes from the edge of one face by pressure or by light percussion and then turning the point over to get the other edge and face. After several resharpenings the blade will become more concave. Some specimens were resharpened so many times that they came to resemble drills instead of knives.

Many archaeologists and collectors believe that the notched Archaic bevels were hafted on short handles and used as knives. It is also possible that some bevels may have served a double purpose, the Daltons in particular. If they were hafted on a foreshaft they could be used on a spear or they could be removed from the longer shaft and used for butchering after the kill was made.

Larger Thebes points like the one illustrated in Fig. 109 have deep, square bottomed notches, indicative of the double flake notching technique. Two flakes are removed side by side as the notch advances, instead of the usual single flake, Fig. 110-A. This helps to prevent hinging in that if one flake fails you have a second chance with the other. Also on wider points, a shoulder is worked into the corners of the base, so the notches will penetrate deeper, Fig. 110-B. Then the stem will be narrower and the point will have a more balanced appearance. This also aids in hafting and was practiced to a varying degree on other beveled types and some dovetails.

Special Notched Points. There are two types that I know of that are found in the Ohio-Indiana area that are very difficult to notch by pressure; they are the "dogleg" notched bevel, Fig. 112, and the E-notched or expanded notched bevel, Fig. 113 & 114. Because the notches go in and curve up or expand out their bottoms are not easily reached by regular pressure flaking. The two techniques that I use on these points are indirect percussion using a 16 penny nail as a punch and straight-in pressure using my steel tipped notching tool.

Both of these techniques will allow you to cut the notches by chipping in, then turning and going up toward the tip. E-notches are a modified form of the dogleg. This modification is accomplished by expanding the notch downward after the upward cut is finished, Fig. 115. The basal cut is always done last in order to lessen the pressure on the ears. Breakage of

FIG. 109. Old Thebes point, found in North-Central Ohio which may have been last used as a scraper. Note the bevel on the left hand edge.

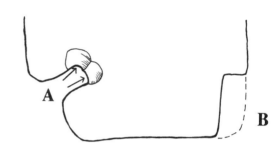

FIG. 110. (A) Double flake notch and (B) shoulder.

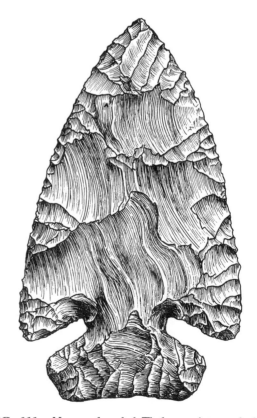

FIG. 111. New, unbeveled Thebes point made by the author. Old un-used specimens such as this are rare.

FIG. 113

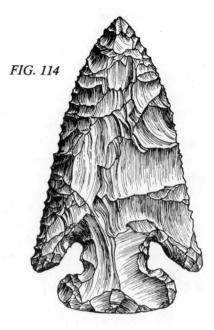

FIG. 114

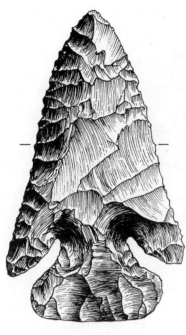

FIG. 112

FIG. 112. Dogleg bevel or Lost lake point. Note the cross-section showing bevel.

FIG. 113. This E-notch was made using a nail punch. It has very fine notches with narrow entries.

FIG. 114. Cruder, pressure notched E-notch.

FIG. 115. Sequence for notching E-notches.

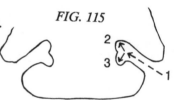

FIG. 115

the basal ears or the barbs is a real headache when making these points.

No matter what method you use for notching the base has to be thinned to at least a 5/1 width to thickness ratio. A 6/1 or 7/1 will definitely assure good results if the knapper does his part. Snapping of the barbs or ears is often the result of excessive force being used to notch a base that is too thick.

Now, for modern flint knappers, indirect percussion with the nail punch is by far the easiest way I have found to do E-notches and other deep notched points. It not only gives you control, but will produce finer, more delicate notches than those found on the majority of aboriginal specimens, Fig. 113.

The 16 penny nail used for notching is between 1 & 1/4" to 1 & 1/2" long and is filed to a long taper with the point radius being about 1/32". This produces a notch entry about 1/8" wide. The point to be notched is laid on the pad on the leg. The left hand rests on the piece holding it down and the nail is held between thumb and forefinger. Before striking the point of the tool is placed firmly, but not hard, down on a spot 1/16" up from the edge for a start. As the notching proceeds with alternate removals placement will have to be closer to the edge in order to prevent an oversized cone. An oversized cone will greatly enlarge the notch beyond that which is desired or, worse yet, split the base off. The angle at the start is between 10 and 20 degrees off

perpendicular (70 to 80 degrees from the center plane). After a flake or two, the tool will be held closer to 90 degrees. This will result in a clean cone and also helps prevent splitting and stacking in the notch.

The blows are dealt with a small antler billet: one that is too short for service as a percussor is about right. The strike should be fairly fast, but light and rebounding, so only the tip of the tool is driven through. Just enough to detach the flake but not enough to wedge in and cause breakage. When using this method I do not abrade in the notches because this thickens the edge causing me to place the tool too high. Abrading is only done after the notch is completed. When pressure flaking notches, especially with a wedge-shaped tool, a small amount of abrading is helpful.

For pressure notching, regular and straight-in, I use the same size nail mounted in an old billet with about 1" sticking out. It is sharpened the same as the punch and the placement above the edge at the start is about the same and continues to be about 1/16" or a little less as the work progresses.

Because both the wedge-shaped and pointed flakers hang up on the barbs when making special notched points a change in technique is required here. After flaking the entries by regular pressure notching as described in Chapter 6 the piece is laid on a thick pad on the work bench. The tool is then taken in both hands and pushed almost straight down at angles of 70-90 degrees. It takes quite a bit of strength to do this. Control leaves something to be desired because sometimes you'll have to rock the tool a bit or lunge at it to get it to go. And when it goes the whole point of the pressure flaker may go through the notch because you won't be able to recover quick enough to stop it. When this happens it opens the notches up more than if it had been done by indirect percussion, Fig. 114.

The case for aboriginal use of straight-in pressure is pretty strong and "strong" is the key word here. The average prehistoric Indian, because of the physical demands of his life style, was probably on the average, stronger than we are today. So he could control his notching tool with greater ease. After examining many originals I believe copper was used for some flaker tips. This metal probably came from the upper Great Lakes area and was work hardened by hammering so that the tool was almost as stiff as mild steel.

Dovetails. The secret to making these fine Archaic points lies in the skillful combination of percussion and pressure that forms a very smooth and regular scar pattern. The wider percussion scars are narrowed by the removal of long pressure flakes from their junctures. Keeping symetry in mind, the point was carefully finished, notched, and the hafting area heavily ground. An asymetrical dovetail will either be damaged or resharpened.

Dovetails are found in three basic varieties that are mostly associated with geographical areas within their range of distribution: the Ohio button base dovetail, Fig. 116, The Indiana-Kentucky type, Fig. 117, and the Illinois-Missouri type, Fig. 118. Though they vary in shape of blade and base, their cross-sections at the center are fairly thick with W/T ratios of 4/1 the norm. These points were used as heavy duty, all purpose knives and the blades were beefed up for strength, yet they taper nicely to very thin bases and sharp points.

FIG. 116

FIG. 117

FIG. 118

Woodland Points. What I call the Woodland percussion style was probably developed during the Middle Archaic where it was used to shape preforms for Thebes points and other types from that period. This style remained in use from then on throughout the entire Eastern Woodland region of the U.S. Its greatest attribute is that of economy. By no other method that I know can one produce a serviceable biface while spending the least amount of time, effort, and material. After making thousands of points I have found that this method can be used to make any size biface, but the real challenge is making the large, super thin ones. Though randomly flaked, some of these points can be real works of art, especially when the surface configurations, cross-sections, and spacing of scars is strictly controlled. Such uniformity gives the illusion of parallel flaking on a large scale. The points illustrated are: the Turkeytail from the Late Archaic-Early Woodland, Fig. 119; and an Ohio Hopewell from the Middle Woodland, Fig. 120.

FIG. 119   FIG. 120

CLOSING COMMENTS

All of the points shown in this book and on its cover, except where noted, were made by the author. What you see is the result of many years of practice and experimentation. The dagger illustrated on this page, though complex as it is, was created through precise and ordered application of the three basic techniques of percussion, indirect percussion and pressure.

The quality and accuracy of your replicas will depend upon observation and research, which leads to a determination of what techniques were used, how they were applied, in what order, as well as any variations or peculiarities that may be inherent to the process. Keeping this in mind the novice knapper should begin with the smallest or the easiest types: birdpoints and small dart points or even some flake and blade tools. After confidence and competence is gained one can move onto bigger and more complex pieces.

The rate at which you learn is directly linked to the amount of time you spend in practice and your aptitude for manual skills. The above can be offset somewhat by visiting knap-ins and sessions of intensive training with a good instructor. You don't necessarily have to go to a master. Another neophyte who has just learned the technique you are trying to grasp may actually be a better teacher because the way he learned it will still be fresh in his mind. This leads to an enthusiasm, willingness, and patience that the long practiced may not have.

The text was designed to teach the basics of biface knapping as it was and is still practiced in North America. As you have seen, heavy emphasis was placed on percussion flaking because most of the preforms for the major point types were made using this technique. Full understanding of this process is absolutely necessary if one wishes to become a good all around knapper. However, this book also documents one man's way of doing things. Your choice of tools and holding positions may vary from mine, your physical type will also be different, so there will have to be some variation and compensation on the themes I have set forth.

Now I realize that after reading this book for the first time it may appear to be very complex, especially for those who have had no formal training in either archaeology or flint knapping. However, you must realize that this is a multi-layered text that builds upon itself, and the novice should not expect to understand everything all at once. As you progress and gain experience you should return to these pages from time to time and more will be revealed as you are ready for it.

Everytime I learn to make a new point type I always go back to my library and check out the literature. I study what specimens I can find, borrow, or get casts of. Then it's back to the basics in an attempt to fine tune and reorder them in the sequence that will produce that type.

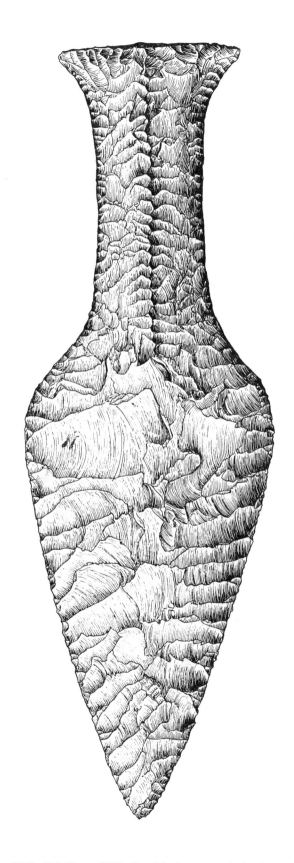

FIG. 121. Type IV-D Danish dagger made by the author from colorful Crescent chert. Also see the photograph on the back cover.

BIBLIOGRAPHY

Bailey, Bruce
1980 A letter in *Flintknappers' Exchange,* Vol. 3, No. 2.

Bordaz, Jaques
1970 *Tools of the Old and New Stone Age,* The Natural History Press, Garden City, New York.

Bordes, Francois
1968 *The Old Stone Age,* World University Library, McGraw-Hill Book Co., New York.

Bradley, Bruce A.
1979 Slotted Block Support, *Flintknappers' Exchange,* Vol. 2, No. 1.

Britt, Claude Jr.
1968 A Geological Classification of Flint, *Ohio Archaeologist,* Vol. 18, No. 2.

Burroughs, Edgar Rice
1914 *The Beasts of Tarzan.* Ballantine Books, New York.

Callahan, Errett
1979 The Basics of Biface Knapping in the Eastern Fluted Point Tradition, A Manual for Flintknappers and Lithic Analysts, *Archaeology of Eastern North America,* Vol. 7, No. 1.

Flenniken, J. Jeffrey and Ervan G. Garrison
1975 Thermally Altered Novaculite and Stone Tool Manufacturing Techniques, *Journal of Field Archaeology,* Vol. 2, No. 1-2.

Hamilton, F.M.
1980 *Colonial Frontier Guns,* The Fur Press, Chadron, Nebraska.

Hester, Thomas R.
1978 *Archaeological Studies of Mesoamerican Obsidian,* Ballens Press, Socorro, New Mexico.

Howell, F. Clark
1965 *Early Man,* Time, Inc., New York.

Kalin, Jeffrey
1981 Flintknapping and Silicosis, *Flintknappers' Exchange,* Vol. 4, No. 2.

Patterson, L.W.
1978 Practical Heat Treating of Flint, *FlintKnappers' Exchange,* Vol. 1, No. 3.

Patterson, L.W.
1981 Fracture Force Changes from Heat Treating and Edge Grinding, *Flintknappers' Exchange,* Vol. 4, No. 3.

Patterson, L.W.
1981 Comments on Pressure Flaking Methods, *Flintknappers' Exchange,* Vol. 4, No. 3.

Purdy, Barbara A. and H.K. Brooks
1971 Thermal Alteration of Silica Minerals: An Archaeological Approach, *Science,* Vol. 173.

Rick, John Winfield
1978 *Heat Altered Cherts of the Lower Illinois Valley* Northwestern Archaeological Program of Prehistorical Records, No. 2

Sollberger, J.B. and L.W. Patterson
1976 Prismatic Blade Replication, *American Antiquity,* Vol. 4, No. 4.

Waldorf, D.C.
1984 *The Art of Flint Knapping, 3rd Edition.* Mound Builder Books, Branson, Missouri.

Waldorf, D.C
1987 *Story in Stone,* Mound Builder Books, Branson.

Zim, Herbert S. and Paul R. Shaffer
1957 *Rocks and Minerals,* Golden Press, New York.

Our special thanks to these people who contributed their time and expertise:

Jack Holland
Paul Grote
Michael Stafford
Larry Scheiber
Kenny Wallace